Want to Be Considered for the Next Edition of Dog Joy?

If you want to participate in the next edition of
Dog Joy to share your dog rescue story and
promote a local dog rescue organization, please
visit our website. Profits from the sale of Dog Joy
books go directly to supporting local dog
rescues featured in the books.

www.DogJoyBook.com

dog joy

Amazing Stories of the Indescribable
Love Only a Rescued Dog Can Give

Caroline Capuzzi

ISBN: 978-1-7325127-3-3

Printed in the United States

On the cover: Mona-Lisa (see chapter #2)

Published by Dog Joy Books
091018

Dog Joy Books is the publisher of a unique type of fundraising books for dog rescues and shelters. Our books are designed to help spread the word of the importance, value and need for local non-profit animal rescues. Visit www.DogJoyBooks.com for more information on how you can publish your own Dog Joy book for your organizations.

This book is dedicated to all the extraordinary
people who dedicate their time and money to
helping dogs in need around the world.

Contents

A Father's Foreword

During a hot summer day in July of 2018, my daughter Caroline and I were swimming in our pool and trying to cajole our rescue dog, Stella (who you will read more about shortly), into joining us in the pool.

Stella, who apparently had zero interest in swimming, teased us by running close to the edge and then darting away as soon as we thought she would make the jump. After a few futile minutes, Stella got bored and laid down on the deck, content to simply watch us.

Caroline and I began to discuss the big and loving impact Stella has had on our family in the seven months since we adopted her. She also reminded me that I was initially against adopting her and of my reservations of getting a "rescue dog."

She was right. Back then, I was hesitant to consider rescuing a dog, mainly because of my lack of awareness and knowledge of dog adoption. While I have always had a dog ever since I was a kid, my family purchased puppies from local breeders.

I admitted to Caroline I was wrong, and that my initial reaction was based on ignorance. I then made the comment, "I bet there are a lot of other people like me. Wouldn't it be cool to share our Stella story with the hope it would inspire others to consider adopting their next four-legged family member?"

We began brainstorming different ideas when I told her about a book I published back in 2008 for a local non-profit organization that helped disadvantaged high school students get into college. I told her how by simply having the students write short stories about the impact of the organization and then putting them together in a short book format, we were able to raise over $100,000 using the book as the keystone of a fundraising campaign.

Caroline then asked me a really smart question... "Can't we do the same thing for dogs?"

For as long as I can remember, Caroline has always loved animals and has been actively involved in taking care of our pets since she was a little kid. Her first "real job" was working at a local animal hospital where she cared for the dogs who were boarding there while their owners were traveling. She loves animals and they love her.

Within the hour, the idea behind Dog Joy was formed while floating under a hot July sun. I reminded Caroline that while publishing a book would be a great experience for her and help her differentiate herself when it came time to apply for college, the big reason behind the book would be to donate <u>100% of the profits</u> to help support local dog rescues. As of the time I am writing this, we have raised almost $3,000 and are hoping to go even higher.

I also thought it would be a neat father-daughter project to work on together, and secretly I was hoping it would be a constructive project to work on during her summer break (and give her a break from her electronic gadgets).

The book you hold in your hands is the result of my daughter's love of dogs and desire to help those dogs that desperately need our collective help. I am proud of her for seeing this through, and while we had a few of the types of "interactions" you might expect between a father and 17 year old daughter, my wife and I could not be more proud of her. I hope in the years to come, she will look back at this effort as something meaningful and important.

I hope you find these stories fun, emotional and inspiring. I can tell you first-hand I got goosebumps and a bit choked-up while reading them. It's truly amazing how rescue dogs change lives as they share their unique type of love and bonding with their "forever families." I know I am a rescue dog convert and am embarrassed by my initial hesitation to open my heart to a rescue dog.

While the monetary donation is important and will help a lot of worthy dogs, our real hope with Dog Joy is it will inspire others to consider adopting a dog from their local animal shelter. With this in mind, please share Dog Joy with your friends and family with your own personal words of experience and encouragement. You can purchase additional copies at **www.DogJoyBook.com** and if you're interested, learn how you could be in the next edition of Dog Joy. Don't forget 100% of the profits of this book goes to supporting local dog rescue organizations featured in Dog Joy.

Finally, as you read through this collection of stories, please realize each chapter was contributed by an individual who has their own writing and communication style. The folks you are about to meet are not professional writers or storytellers, but they all have an important story to tell. We did not do heavy editing because we wanted the true essence of each author's story to shine through in their own voice, and while we did extensive proofreading and grammar-checking I am sure some readers may find errors (if you do, please email us at friend@dogjoybook.com). Whatever you do, please don't allow these small imperfections to take away from the big idea behind this book.

Mike Capuzzi (Caroline's dad)
www.MikeCapuzzi.com

Thank You !

I would to thank the following Dog Joy contributing authors for making this collection of wonderful dog rescue stories a reality. Their time, effort and stories are appreciated. I would like to acknowledge Mr. Balbach for designing the cover and Mr. Brakefield for helping to proof-read Dog Joy.

Bob Arnold	**Lynn Horner Baker**
Madison & Brian Bacak	**David Lee**
Mark S. Balbach	**Jennifer Lee**
Phil Brakefield	**Francine E. Love**
Mike Caldwell	**Sandra McGuckin**
Dr. Ivan Carney	**Katherine Molnar-Kimber**
Dwight O. Chandler	**Kris Murray**
Victoria L. Collier	**Sherman Ragland**
Nina Drumsta	**Steve Sipress**
Leslie Elhai	**Amanda White**
Jeff Giagnocavo	**MaryBeth Yannessa**
Michael Gravette	**Frank Zuniga**

In addition to the contributing authors, several others supported the Dog Joy effort by pre-ordering books. Thank you to these generous individuals:

Sakuma Avery

Brian & Tina Bergh + Maddi

Lisa Flagg

Pat Flynn

Mike & Debi Gifford

Karen & Bill Glazer

Bill Greer

Bill Harrison

Lucy & Jeff Hunter

Lynn & Bob Hunter

Dean Killingbeck

Jenna Muth + Kate

Paul Nolte

Kris O'Connor

Linda & David Peluso

Matthew Petruso

Michael & Jennifer Phillips + Beau

Paw Prints at Kitchen Kettle Village

Diane Souder

Michael Steigman

Maureen & Frank Tibbs + Finnegan

Barbara Wong

Finally, I would like to thank my dad and mom for helping and encouraging me to create Dog Joy. I could not have done it without your love and assistance.

The Rescue Organizations

I asked each contributing author to highlight a non-profit dog rescue, shelter or organization which supports dog rescue and adoption. As you will soon read, not everybody in Dog Joy adopted their dog. In some cases, they found their dog or he/she was given to them, but in all cases a dog's life was saved and changed forever.

If you live in an area where one of these organizations is located, by all means please visit them and let them know the contributing author and Dog Joy sent you there.

Animal Friends of the Valleys, Wildomar, CA

Animal House Project, Pottstown, PA

Animal House Shelter, Huntley, IL

Animal Protection Society of Caswell County, Yanceyville, NC

Austin Pets Alive!, Austin, TX

Baltimore Animal Rescue and Care Shelter, Baltimore, MD

Berks Animal Rescue League, Birdsboro, PA

Best Friends Animal Society, Kanab, UT

BullyWag, Douglasville, GA

Chicagoland Dog Rescue, Chicago, IL

Dog Town Rescue, Colmar, PA

Don't Bully Us Rescue, Philadelphia, PA

First Coast No More Homeless Pets, Jacksonville, FL

Fulton County Animal Services, Atlanta, GA

Greenmore Farm Animal Rescue, West Grove, PA

Homeless Pet Foundation, Marietta, GA

Hope for Paws, Los Angeles, CA

Huron Valley Humane Society, Ann Arbor, MI

Lake Erie Labrador Retriever Rescue, Bath, OH

Lawrence County Humane Society, New Castle, PA

Les Anges Gardiens Des Animaux, Quebec, Canada

Linda Ann's Greyhound Adoption, Allentown, PA

Livingston County Humane Society, Howell, MI

North Shore Animal League America, Port Washington, NY

Rocky Mountain Lab Rescue, Denver, CO

Stray Network Animal Rescue, Memphis, TN and Glenside, PA

True Blue Animal Rescue, Brenham, TX

Useless Bay Sanctuary, Seahurst, WA

Introduction

The American Society for the Prevention of Cruelty to Animals (ASPCA) estimates that nationally, U.S. animal shelters have an intake of 6.5 million companion animals each year – roughly 3.3 million are dogs. Although the numbers of these animals entering shelters and being euthanized have declined, there are still an estimated 670,000 dogs euthanized every year. The increase in adoptions and return of animals to their owners has aided that decrease.

When I was younger, I wanted to volunteer at the local SPCA, but at the time, I was too young to volunteer. At the same time, even though I wasn't yet 16-years old, I wrote a personal letter to several local animal hospitals to see if they would hire a 15-year old. Only one responded, the West Chester Animal Hospital, which also happens to be the veterinary practice we took our last dog, Zoe, and our current dog, Stella, to. They told me to follow-up with them when I turned 16 and was able to work.

In late spring of 2017, I was hired to work in the kennel at West Chester Animal Hospital. There are so many rescue dogs that board there – and besides reading stories on the Internet, or from the contributors in this book – I think being surrounded by them has been one of the biggest eye-openers about rescuing dogs.

Many of them have similar demeanors and personalities, and it pains me to think about the similarity of the toxic backgrounds they came from. I never have really believed the stereotypes and stigmas surrounding certain breeds, such as bully breeds, but working with them would have completely quashed any assumptions or opinions I could have had prior to working there. Before taking adoption out of consideration, please read more about it, and meet with adoptable dogs in your area, to see if you could, in fact, provide them with a second chance.

My primary goal for Dog Joy is to help educate and inspire readers to adopt their next pets. If more and more people continue to adopt, the aforementioned statistics will continue to decrease, and the amount of deserving animals being placed in their forever homes will increase.

The other important goal I have is to raise money to help support dog rescues around the country, and as I write this we have already sold over $5,000 worth of books. I was initially going to donate this money to a national organization that supports dog rescues, but after seeing all the amazing stories you are about to read, I changed my mind and decided to award several of the rescue organizations featured in Dog Joy a donation. You can read about these donations at www.DogJoyBook.com.

Finally, I hope people who were hesitant and apprehensive about adopting a rescue dog prior to reading this book learn those are factors to embrace, and not reasons to hold themselves back from saving a dog's life. I know my family now cannot imagine life without our rescued dog Stella who you will soon meet.

The diverse, passionate and emotional stories within this book will more than likely change any preconceived notions you may have about rescuing a dog. I hope Dog Joy can accomplish that, and I hope you can experience or re-experience the indescribable love only a rescued dog can give. Thank you.

Caroline and Stella Capuzzi

Stella

Stella was adopted from Greenmore Farm Animal Rescue in West Grove, Pennsylvania. Greenmore Farm Animal Rescue is a 501(c)(3) rescue for animals in need of shelter, food, and health/ medical care while the rescue's adoption team works to find their forever homes. They even have a volunteer pilot, Jack, who transports dogs to rescues he works with. Stella was flown from a high-kill shelter in Tennessee to Greenmore Farm Animal Rescue, courtesy of Jack.

www.GreenmoreRescue.org

My Other Teenage Sister

On December 2, 2017, my family and I rescued our dog Stella. The week before, we were on vacation in Colorado for Thanksgiving. My mom spent downtime from skiing looking at animal rescue sites, trying to find a dog in need of a home close to where we live in Pennsylvania. A young Australian Shepherd/Border Collie mix named Elvie caught her eye, and when we got back home, she filled out an online application to qualify for adopting Elvie and scheduled a time to meet her at Greenmore Farm Animal Rescue.

I worked that day and left early to go home so we could drive over to meet her. I work in a kennel that is a part of the highly-praised veterinary practice West Chester Animal

Hospital, where we used to take our German Shepherd, Zoe. My shift on that Saturday was nostalgic, as it was one year ago on this very date when we had to put Zoe down there. This made meeting and getting Elvie seem like fate.

We went an entire year to the date without a dog, and after always having one since before I was born, there was undoubtedly a void in our family. There's just something about having a dog that gives a sense of completion. Our only pet during the span of being dog-less was our Guinea pig, Fudge. Going from having a dog and two Guinea pigs to no dog and one Guinea pig was very disconsolate. I started working in a kennel a little over six months after Zoe was put down, so it was good to be surrounded by all the animals there, what with only having one to come home to. It was, and still is, also good to have the exposure of working with so many different dogs all in the same place – purebreds, mutts, old dogs, young dogs.

Our first days with Stella were so exciting, my family debated names for the first few until we all collectively agreed on Stella. We had named our German Shepherd "Zoe" from the character in Sesame Street, since my sister and I were only two and three, and we loved that show. My mom had sent a text in a group chat with my sister and I, as we were in school, saying "Stella? = star in Italian" and that's where her name originated from.

This was our first rescue dog, so we were anxious to see how she fit into our family. While Greenmore guessed her age to be between one and two years old, it quickly became apparent Stella was still a puppy. At first, she was timid and waking up early, but after a few weeks of getting used to her "forever home," Stella settled in nicely.

As I write this, Stella acts just like a teenager. She goes to bed late and sleeps in late. If she wakes up when my sister, parents or I get up early, she goes outside to go the bathroom, comes in and eats breakfast, then goes back to sleep, either on her bed or on her "throne" – a chair in our sunroom that she deemed hers. She will continue to sleep sometimes until noon!

There are times when we will call her name or try and get her to go outside or say hi to someone she doesn't quite know yet, and she can be just as adamant as a teenager – she will blatantly ignore us, or just stay where she is, or bark and growl her head off. Similar reactions to those of a typical teenager who doesn't want to do something!

Stella also is friends with another rescue dog about the same size and age as her, one house down the street. Every time we take her for a walk, she tries to turn into the family's driveway, and looks around for her friend in the yard. They literally hang out just like teenagers!

One of the strangest things about her, which is yet again a teenager-like quality, is her routine tendency to get very energetic at night. During the day, she usually just lays around, either inside or outside, but around nine o'clock at night, she "wakes up" and is a literal ball of energy wanting to play and "wrestle" with my dad.

Stella is just like a lot of teenagers these days – sleeping in late, not doing much during the day and going out at night. Now you see why I call her my other teenage sister!

It was and still is so fun finding all her quirks. If you get a dog straight from a breeder when it's only eight weeks old or so, they don't have preconceived notions or behaviors like a rescue dog does. Puppies from breeders obviously do not endure the hardships and tribulations most rescue dogs do, so with a rescue dog, there is a lot more you must learn about and accommodate to with their personality.

Our experiences learning about and with Stella have been so fun and surprising with the indescribable love only a rescued dog can give.

About Caroline Capuzzi

Caroline Capuzzi is a senior at B. Reed Henderson High School in West Chester, Pennsylvania. Ever since she was little, she has had a passion for all animals, but especially dogs. Her love for dogs was the reason she reached out to several local animal hospitals when she was 15 years old, inquiring if they had job openings for a high school student. Dr. Brenda Perkins, owner of the West Chester Animal Hospital, responded and instructed Caroline to follow up with her when she turned 16. She did and got her first job caring for the dogs that board at the hospital's kennel. Dog Joy has reignited her passion for writing.

You can contact Caroline by email at caroline@dogjoybook.com.

Mona-Lisa

Mona-Lisa was adopted at Linda Ann's Greyhound Adoption, which is an all-volunteer, non-profit 501(c)(3) registered adoption group devoted to the welfare of retired racing Greyhounds. Their home base is in Allentown, Pennsylvania. They serve the needs for Greyhounds in and around the Lehigh Valley area.

Each of their Greyhounds is first placed in a foster home where they learn how to adapt to living in a home. They then will find the best homes for as many dogs of this very deserving breed as possible. Linda Ann's provides as much support and education as the owner/prospective owner wants and needs before, during and after the adoption. They strive to make the transition as smooth as possible for both the Greyhound and the family.

www.LindasGreys.com

I Just Wanted a Buddy

I just wanted a buddy when I found and brought home my first rescue dog... but I received so much more.

I was 27 when I stepped into the Chester County SPCA, just before Easter that year. I was an energetic young man – successful and happy in many aspects of my life – yet something was missing. I had known for a while that I needed a friend to come home to, to share my life with, and hopefully give her a better life than she once had – speaking of the four-legged variety that barks, obviously.

Naya, a Shepherd/Sheltie/Husky mix, and I found each other. She became my baby and my everything. As full as my life was with work and friends, coming home to her, running, playing, and road trips made me complete. Still, as "perfect" as everything was, I felt something was missing – a companion for her, for when I was not always around. Researching K-9 personality types, and still wanting to rescue an animal in need, I went back to the same SPCA where I got Naya. All the dogs were quiet... then I heard a lone wolf howl from the end of the kennel. I walked to the back and there sat a malnourished, young Siberian Huskey, Isis. As I approached her, she was howling, as Huskies do, and pawing the door at me – it was love at first sight.

Naya and Isis became quick buddies – inseparable in every way. We went on many adventures and traveled around the United States. Having them as part of my life made me blossom as an individual so much more than I could have imagined... from the countless people I met (who wanted to meet them), to learning and understanding about specific breeds, not just theirs. The list goes on of how having a rescue dog can profoundly change your life.

Naya and Isis became my children for the following 15 years. I lost Isis first to cancer in 2016, then Naya to another cancerous illness in 2017. I was devastated. I vowed to myself, "I am never getting another dog ever again. I am going to travel, do this and that, etc."

After going through the grieving process, it became clear to me after some time that I genuinely needed to have a dog to share my time with. After analyzing my life, researching breeds and identifying the best breed match for my lifestyle now (very different from 15 years prior) I concluded a Greyhound would be the perfect fit.

Fortunately, retired racing Greyhounds, all around the country, are very much in need of homes. I was very blessed – the rescue group I reached out to, Linda Ann's Greyhound Adoption, was extremely helpful and knowledgeable. I found my now sidekick, forever companion Mona-Lisa (shown on the cover photo of this book.) I was additionally blessed by meeting who I now refer to as "Aunt Kathi & Uncle Bob", Mona's foster parents, who are now my best friends. When I go out of town, Mona-Lisa gets to stay with them and their wonderful Greyhounds (so it's like a vacation of play and love for her) and I couldn't imagine leaving her in anyone else's care.

Greyhounds are a breed in and of themselves, unique, but if you can give them the focus during their transition time, and learn and understand their uniqueness, it's a phenomenal partnership that you can forge. My newest rescue, and my forever companion Mona-Lisa is a perfect fit for me and my lifestyle. Yes, like any relationship – human or animal – there is a learning process, give and take, getting out of comfort zones, but once you move beyond that, the rewards are bountiful.

Rescuing a dog and giving him or her a brand-new life with the right commitment on your part will always be a win-win. I know, for myself, I could not imagine where I would be or what my life would be like without ever having had shared it with a rescue dog.

Our rescue animals are not the whole of our lives, but they make our lives whole.

About Mark S. Balbach

Mark S. Balbach is the lead designer and social media marketing consultant for The Million Dollar Solution, bringing more than 20 years of experience in marketing and creative services to help guide elder law and estate planning attorneys in their marketing efforts. He brings a wide array of creative skills to The Million Dollar Solution in both print and online design. He has worked with entrepreneurs, small agencies as well as large corporations such as Harley-Davidson, Hilton Hotels, Glazer Kennedy's Insider's Circle and Comcast.

When not designing, you'll find Mark devoting most of his time to his retired Greyhound, Mona-Lisa. He is an avid lover of the outdoors, enjoys hiking, running and capturing stunning images of nature and experimenting with astro-photography.

You can contact Mark at mstephbalbach@gmail.com.

Roxy

Roxy was rescued from the Chicagoland Dog Rescue. Chicagoland Dog Rescue is a totally volunteer-based, shelter-less rescue. It is a 501(c)(3) non-profit organization that has been dedicated to rescuing, socializing and placing homeless dogs – regardless of breed, size or age - into permanent loving homes for the last 20 years.

www.ChicagolandDogRescue.org

.

Da Rox

We could not have come into each other's lives at a more perfect time. We saw one another for the first time at the same exact moment. Roxy was terrified, disoriented, in ill health, and very much in need of someone to love her. And I had forgotten how to embrace the need to be needed.

She was a 100-pound, pure-bred Newfie who was at least 30 pounds underweight, and I was emotionally shut down following the loss a few weeks earlier of my beloved four-year-old German Shepherd, Terra, to leukemia.

So, there we were, sizing each other up, and I guess that despite our challenges, we both liked what we saw. As a favor to the president of our organization, Chicagoland Dog

Rescue, I agreed to foster Roxy for a while, because we had no other place for her to go.

"OK, kiddo. We got this. You're going to stay with me for a while."

In hindsight, I remember how easily she fell into step beside me as we headed for my car, and I suspect she knew long before I did she would be staying with me for more than a while. We settled immediately into an easy rhythm of sharing our lives. We played goofy games with each other, and she couldn't wait to go to work with me every day. As time went on, she assumed the mantle of our rescue's super-star ambassador dog and became quickly known as Da Rox. It was quite a mantle. It had to fit her 160-pound frame!

For the next nine years, she tirelessly appeared at fund-raising functions, posed for calendars, taught our youngest foster puppies their manners, and endured adolescents, both canine and human, as they climbed all over her, testing her limitless patience. And she showed our hope-starved senior rescues that she had once been just like them, and to never lose hope. And, oh my goodness, Da Rox literally travelled the world without ever leaving Illinois. No matter where we went or what we did, folks insisted on selfies with Da Rox, which they would immediately share. She became a marquee star in China, Japan, Germany, Italy and even Boone, North Carolina. Her humble confidence and easy charisma won over every single heart she ever encountered.

Then on April 5, 2017, my beautiful 27-year-old daughter, Jamie, died from a drug overdose. For many days afterwards, Roxy did not...would not...leave my side. She shadowed my every movement and made sure that she was always in contact with me, in some way. She knew that I really didn't want to be here anymore.

But she would quietly lay her big bear head in my lap, and look at me with those eyes that were always more human than dog, as if to say, "Ok, Kiddo. We got this. You're going to stay with me for a while."

Quite simply...she saved my life. And against all odds, though completely unimaginable, after Jamie's death my bond with Da Rox grew even stronger.

She really was my soulmate. And I was hers. Don't ask me to explain that.

It just...was.

Then, in mid-August 2017, she suddenly became ill and couldn't keep food or water down, so of course off to the vet we went. What was originally diagnosed as the canine version of diverticulitis was eventually determined to be cancer of her intestines. The doctors told us that at her age, surviving surgery would be a 50/50 proposition at best, and even if she pulled through, her quality of life would be severely compromised.

So, she and I talked it over, right then and there at the vet's, and as heartbreaking as it was, decided it was time she should set out for the Rainbow Bridge.

We spent another couple of hours together reviewing the joys and challenges of our lives together, agreeing that there could have never been a sweeter relationship than the one we shared. Then it was time to say goodbye, and the vet came in with the needle that would send her on her next journey.

She greeted him with a wag of that mighty tail. She was just that way. I held her big bear head in my lap and said, "OK, kiddo, we got this."

With a final loving look at me she sighed deeply and slipped peacefully away. My life will never be the same without Da Rox in it. But it will always be better because she was...

About Phil Brakefield

Phil Brakefield is a serial marketing strategist, writer, speaker, apparel and promotional products expert who began learning promotion and marketing techniques while traveling with rock groups like Led Zeppelin, Three Dog Night, Jimi Hendrix, Elvis, The Moody Blues, John Denver and many others. Phil was also a Golden Gloves boxer, professional soccer player, model and appeared in the movie "Semi-Tough" with Burt Reynolds, Kris Kristofferson and Jill Clayburgh. In recent years Phil has been very involved in dog rescue work as a board member of Chicagoland Dog Rescue.

You can contact Phil on his Facebook page or via his LinkedIn profile.

Simba

Simba is the third Labrador Retriever I've rescued. He came to me through Rocky Mountain Lab Rescue, based in Denver, Colorado. Rocky Mountain Lab is a shelter-less rescue, which means it relies 100% on foster homes. Each year they rescue hundreds (if not thousands) of dogs because of all the loving people who help foster these needy dogs.

www.RockyMountainLabRescue.com

Gratitude: Why Rescue Dogs Make the Best Dogs

I have rescued three dogs in my lifetime, and I hope to be able to save a few more lives before mine is done. All three have been Labradors. Simba is my third rescue, the only male, and the only chocolate Lab (the other two were yellow females). It's funny, because I never thought I could find a dog more loyal, easy-going, and loving than my other two. Simba proved me wrong.

As with many rescue dogs, we don't know the specifics of how Simba came to be lost, and what happened to him during this tough time in his life. If only he could speak and tell us his story. Therefore, I'll share his story with you, in as much detail as I know.

Simba is a beautiful male dog. A purebred, he was obviously well-trained and from a home that cared for him. He was raised in the woods of Arkansas outside of Little Rock, where he was found. When he was brought in to the Little Rock vet's office, he was a scrawny, barely surviving, flea-bitten thing that weighed just over 50 pounds. (Today, he weighs nearly 90 pounds! Like many Labs, Simba loves to eat, and he does not like skipping a meal). He had just turned two years old, by the best guess of the vet.

Simba was brought into that Little Rock vet by a "mountain man" sort of guy. A guy who is a hermit and lives in the woods with lots of dogs and strays. He recognized that Simba was a highly trained purebred who could easily get adopted into a good home and have a great life. So, with this story I also would like to thank the mountain man who decided not to keep Simba. Thanks for letting him go so he could fill our family's hearts and lives with love.

The vet in Little Rock was friends with one of the ladies that runs (or is connected to) Rocky Mountain Lab Rescue. They decided to put Simba on a transport and bring him out to Colorado for a new life. I live in the mountains of Colorado, and I had been pre-approved to foster and then adopt a dog by the rescue folks. When they contacted me to see if I wanted to take Simba, I jumped at the chance.

I prepped my family and my home and bought a new crate for Simba. None of my other Labs have been crate-trained, but I wanted Simba to feel comfortable with our four-hour drive back home. On the way to Denver, my transport contact called me. "I hope you didn't bring a crate, because Simba really seems to HATE them." Oh, okay, I thought! Return the crate. Check.

I'll never forget the day I pulled up in the parking lot and saw the transport vehicle arriving. I was so excited I could barely stand it! When I saw Simba for the first time, my heart was so happy. If you can have "love at first sight" with a pup, this was it!

I brought Simba home that day, and he mostly hung out in the back seat on a blanket for the 4-hour drive home. I talked to him a lot, and stopped for walks as much as possible along the way. It was February, so there was a good amount of snow on the ground. He seemed happy and content. He was a joy to be with, from the first minute I saw him.

So, you might be wondering, how could this have happened to such an amazing young male purebred dog that was fully trained and well-adjusted? Why was he lost in the woods? Well, pets do get lost from their owners. They also get abandoned.

After I had Simba a few weeks, I noticed that his rear left leg seemed a bit "off," especially when he went down a flight of stairs. I took him to the vet to get him looked at. He apparently suffered a growth plate injury in his knee, so he essentially stands on his "tip toes" on his rear left leg because his leg did not fully form.

So, this is where the questions come in. Did he get lost from his family, and then get injured somehow while wandering the woods... or... did he get injured and then his owner abandoned him because of the injury? Again, I sure wish Simba could tell us his story, and we would know the real truth about what happened out there in the woods of Arkansas.

At the end of the day, it doesn't really matter. What DOES matter is that Simba and I found each other. Because this dog is the most loyal, loving, wonderful companion that I have ever had.

Here's what I know for sure. Rescue dogs are the best dogs, because they are GRATEFUL to the human that saved them. They have all gone through some sort of tumultuous journey, and when they land in their forever home, they are the happiest and most grateful creatures on earth. They make the best dogs.

About Kris Murray

Kris Murray is President and Founder of Child Care Marketing Solutions, a company dedicated to helping preschool and daycare centers succeed in the areas of business, marketing, operations, staffing, leadership, and personal productivity. Kris and her team have helped thousands of child care center owners and leaders be more successful and live happier, more abundant lives. Kris is the author of two books and the host of the world's largest early learning business conference, the annual Child Care Success Summit. Kris lives in the mountains of Colorado with her two children, Owen and Maeve, and of course, Simba.

Learn more about Kris at www.ChildCare-Marketing.com.

Soli

Stray Network Animal Rescue, in Memphis, Tennessee and Glen-side, Pennsylvania, is a group of dog-loving volunteers who rescue abused, displaced, disposed and unwanted dogs of the mid-south and surrounding areas, specializing in stray pregnant moms and pups, and orphaned puppies. The dogs of Stray Network are housed in foster homes where they are provided with an enormous amount of love and attention. All our animals are spayed or neutered and brought up-to-date on shots before being placed in their new homes. Stray Network is run by professionals who volunteer their time and resources to help save the lives of these animals.

www.StrayNetwork.org

Saved By Soli

I have always been an animal rescuer and advocate. I rescued puppies that were left behind a farmer's market when I was ten. I hid an abandoned baby squirrel under my bed when I was twelve. I even became a vegetarian when I was seventeen, which I have remained till this day. I protested furs and circuses in my twenties. All these acts of escalating animal compassion could not prepare me for what would happen as an adult.

I was living in a small rural town in Pennsylvania with my husband and young twins, and we were very active in our community. I was a team mom for my older children's sports, I organized teen nightclub events promoting a drug and alcohol-free lifestyle. I volunteered at homeless shelters. I really enjoyed my life, and was very content.

However, in May 2012, my husband was offered and accepted a life-changing career opportunity out of state. So, we made the joint decision to uproot, and as a united family we moved to Memphis, Tennessee. We loaded the truck and our then twin three-year-olds, and headed to a state we'd never more than visited once to start our new adventure.

Having just moved there, we were sharing one car until our other vehicle arrived from Pennsylvania. It wasn't a hassle; I enjoyed it, and always took a longer, more scenic route home to explore my new area. Three weeks into our new lives, after the kids and I dropped off my husband, we were on our drive back to our temporary corporate housing. As we exited the ramp, a truck in the opposite lane of traffic from me began to slow down. Not super strange, but as I approached, he appeared to throw something out of his window. My heart sank as I realized this was not just "something" - this was a dog!

I spun my car around and jumped out and began to race toward the injured dog lying in the middle of the six-lane road way. She was alive! She seemed to have a lot of hair loss and was beyond scared. Even though she was injured, she tried to get away from me. I was able to get her, and without thought of potentially being bit, I picked her up and carried her to my minivan. This scared, abused dog was trembling, and her fur smelled like rotten eggs. She had a large tummy that looked bloated. I didn't know if this was from internal injuries or what.

Suddenly, I was freaking out as the gravity of what I had just experienced started to set in. My legs were shaking from pure adrenaline. I called my husband (he was the only other adult in the state of Tennessee I knew at the time) and told him what happened. I told him to ask others in his office about veterinary offices near where I was. One of his coworkers suggested the Germantown Animal Shelter, and that I should take her there in case this dog was dumped, and potentially belonged to someone else. I was certain she didn't have a home, or at least a good one, based on what had just happened, and the overall appearance of her bloated hair loss body. But as advised, I headed toward the shelter.

When I arrived, I was incredibly taken aback by the reaction of the staff. They appeared to not be surprised at all that this occurred, acting as if it was comical for me to have been shocked by it. The animal control officer advised me that it appeared that this dog had mange and was certainly just a stray. He looked at me judgingly, and that we had all potentially been exposed. Mange is very contagious skin mite (not going to lie, I had a mini freak-out then). He also said they were full, and after a required hold time she'd probably be euthanized.

I walked to my car with an incredibly large range of emotions. Heartbreak that a human could intentionally starve/neglect and then toss out a dog like this; fear that she might be put to sleep; fear that my kids and I might get mange; sadness that the animal control worker was so callus about the life of an animal.

After I got home, I showered, prayed and talked to my husband. We decided we would go get this girl in the morning, and give her a home and a better life. The next morning, we went to pick up Soli, and took her to the pet hospital in Germantown, where they diagnosed her with a myriad of parasites, including sarcoptic mange. She had to stay in quarantine for three weeks. That day we opened our hearts and wallets to a rescue dog, and after almost a $2,000 vet bill, we never stopped.

I am now the founder of Stray Network Animal Rescue, and in the years following that first Memphis rescue, we have been able to save over 3,000 dogs from the area. On that fateful day in 2012, people may say I saved Soli's life, but she saved mine, and thousands of others!

About Sandra McGuckin

Sandra McGuckin is the Founder of Stray Network Animal Rescue. Sandra works with several midsouth shelters, animal control officers and volunteers. She spends a lot of time organizing the dogs to be pulled from shelters, personally paying for any associated fees and veterinary care fees, supplying her own vehicle and even money to cover the gas and driver. Having a large network of reputable rescues, humane societies, no-kill shelters and a notable gift of gab, Sandra has been able to make an incredible difference in the midsouth area.

You can contact Sandra at straynetworkrescue@gmail.com.

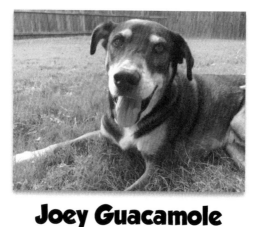

Joey Guacamole

Fulton County Animal Services, located in Atlanta, Georgia, used to be a typical shelter where animals were euthanized if not adopted within a certain time frame. That all changed in 2013 when it was taken over by the LifeLine Animal Project which provides care for homeless animals, pet adoption services and enforcement of the animal control laws in Fulton County, Georgia.

Since taking over management of FCAS and DCAS in 2013, thousands of lives have been saved and adoptions have been increased by 150%! Over 15,000 homeless animals (that's more than 40 a day!) enter their shelters each year. LifeLine's goal is that all healthy and treatable pets leave their shelters alive and find loving homes.

www.FultonAnimalServices.com

The Most Popular Dog on the Block

I said good-bye to my pet soulmate in 1997 due to a human break-up. Ashley Blue, a blue merle Great Dane, was the animal love of my life. After seven years, finishing my undergraduate degree and law school, I was ready to fall in love again.

My good friend Kim and I went on a search one Saturday afternoon. After perusing five shelters, I had almost given up. Kim talked me into visiting one more shelter, Fulton County Animal Services, where animals were put down if not adopted within a certain time frame.

I had never adopted an animal before; rather, I had always purchased them from private individuals. As I walked down row by row of cage after cage, my heart broke more and more. I knew I could not take them all home. My wife had given me strict instructions – a small dog that does not shed a lot.

Turning the corner, I was face to face with two adorable puppies. One looked like a Chow mix (I knew that would be too big when the puppy days were done) and the other a beagle mix. I had owned a beagle once before; happy, hard-headed and only 25 pounds. I asked to take "Pup Pup" out of his cell so I could play with him outside a bit. He was as forlorn as a rainy afternoon. All the pets I had in the past were female, but there was something special in Pup Pup's deep eyes that made me take a chance on adding a male to the family.

When completing the application for adoption, I was told there were two other interested families ahead of me. We all needed to show up on a certain date by 8:00 a.m., not a minute after. Well, the night before adoption day, a hurricane swept through the southeast. The second one in two weeks. I was so afraid it would take hours to detour around all the downed trees blocking my way, that I left at 6:30, for what would normally take 15 minutes.

The damage was not as bad as I had imagined, and we got there super early. The shelter had no electricity due to the storm, and they warned we may not get to adopt any animals that day. I hadn't slept at all the night before, because I was so afraid I would not get to adopt Pup Pup. I had already changed his name to Joey Guacamole. It just had a nice ring to it.

Aside from frequenting the restroom for bowel issues due to nerves, I sat there and panicked each time a person walked into the building, just sure that he or she was there to get Joey. Then it happened. Eight o'clock sharp. I was still the only person in the lobby. Then 8:01. Then 8:02.

Suddenly, at 8:03, a man walked in carrying nothing but a checkbook. The lady behind the glass told him to check in. He did. I walked to the glass and pleaded that I had not been told to check in. The lady smiled and said, "Honey, we know you've been here all morning." I glanced at the log-in, where the man had written he was there at 8:00. That was just not true, so I corrected it to 8:03.

From around the corner, an employee walked straight to the clipboard, reviewed it, and said, "Chris," who stood up eagerly to get Pup Pup. "I'm sorry, you were not here at 8:00." As his shoulders dropped, my heart raced inside, because I knew Joey Guacamole was as good as mine. Thirty minutes later, a woman who had driven all the way to Georgia from Alabama to get Pup Pup showed up, extremely belligerent that she was too late.

On the way home, Joey laid on the front seat and never took his eyes off me. Fourteen years later, we still have staring contests, gratitude and unconditional love for each other. Much to my wife's chagrin, Joey grew to be 58 pounds and sheds terribly.

Joey was there when I brought my twins home from the hospital, taking them under his paws and raising them alongside me. Then, in turn, my children nursed Joey back to health after his knee surgery. Adopting Joey has enriched the lives of so many.

About Victoria L. Collier

Victoria has always been an avid animal lover. During high school, she moved in with a roommate that had five cats and three dogs. Even though Victoria was allergic to cats, she scratched herself each night with their paws to become immune to the allergens. While in the military, she rescued feral kittens, found homes for all of them, and raised one herself. Today in her estate planning, asset protection and elder law practice, Victoria creates pet trusts to protect furry family members when their humans get sick or pass away.

Visit www.TheEstateAndAssetProtectionLawFirm.com.

Cado

Animal House Project, located in Pottstown, Pennsylvania, is a 501(c)(3) 100% volunteer, charitable organization on a mission to help companion pets stay at home and out of animal shelters by providing donated pet food and pet care services to families in financial need. At times, we are the last option for families to keep their companion pets at home. In addition to our Companion Pet Food Program, Animal House Project also operates the Rescue Pet Food Pantry. The Rescue Pet Food Pantry provides larger quantities of food to community-based animal welfare groups, allowing them to shift scarce funds to other needs, such as spay/neuter, vet services, facility improvements and adoption events.

www.AnimalHouseProject.org

Cado's Journey

In December of 2015, Animal House Project received a desperate call from several rescues in rural Georgia needing large quantities of pet food. Under our Rescue Food Pantry Program, we were able to facilitate the request, and 27 pallets of both dog and cat food were sent on a donated 53' tractor trailer to Blackshear, Georgia.

In preparation of the arrival of the truck, Rick Allmon went to the back gate of the farm to open and clear a path, as a tractor trailer had never traversed the dirt road, and there was concern that the load would be too heavy. Right outside the gate, he found a cardboard box, and inside were six newborn puppies that someone had dumped.

Unfortunately, this is a common occurrence in the southern states.

It was never my intent when I agreed to accompany Animal Aid USA on their caravan trip in early January 2016, that I would be coming home with a puppy. In fact, I was strongly advised by my husband that I was not to bring home another dog. You see, we already had two large Akitas (Yoshi and Bella) and two cats that occupied our time, plus we traveled a lot for work.

Karen Talbot of Animal Aid USA runs the transport service from New Jersey down to Blackshear, Georgia, and then back to New Jersey. She invited me along with their group to meet the rescue recipients of the donated cat and dog food. Normally, they send 3-4 vans and one long trailer on their trips, and each van has 2-4 volunteers that switch out driving to make the long journey. We left on a Thursday evening and drove through the night.

Our first stop – Long County Animal Shelter on Friday morning, and my heart was breaking as I was seeing all the dogs that were housed in this county-run kill shelter. I wanted to wrap my arms around all of them and take them home. This was my first boots-on-the-ground look at a kill shelter, and it was not a pleasant sight. From Long County's Facility, we went to All About Animals Rescue, a no-kill animal shelter in Blackshear, Georgia. What a site to see as we arrived – there were dogs and cats everywhere, I literally mean everywhere ... as far as the eyes could see, on the property as well as in the main house.

As we all disembarked from the vans, I was introduced to Rick and Nancy Allmon, as well as to many of the other rescue personnel who had received the 27 pallets of wet and dry dog and cat food. They were so appreciative that in their hour of need, Animal House Project's Program was able to supply the much-needed food, not to mention that our van was packed to the tippy top with lots of treats. As we were walking the property, they shared the story of the Littergate Puppies that were found while they were getting ready for the delivery of the food, and that if not for the arrival of the tractor trailer, the pups would have surely died in the cardboard box. Nancy told me there were five boys and one girl, and, in my head, I kept saying to myself, "I am not allowed to bring a puppy home," as she took me to the puppy compound.

Everyone reminded me of my "No Puppy Resolve." We reached the compound and my heart melted. I picked up the female and she barely gave me a second look, then I picked up one of the smaller males and still no interest. I had just said to Nancy – this is great, I am in the clear, but happy that the delivery of the food saved the puppies. "Not so fast," I guess, was the answer as we started to walk out –

my compadre told me to look down at my leg, as I had a passenger who looked like one big tick attached to my calf. He was hanging onto my calf for dear life, and as I looked down, he had the most soulful sad eyes, and my resolve melted. I reached down and picked him off my leg and he snuggled so close in my arms that it was love at first sight for both of us. I knew at that moment he was going home with me. The tag around his neck said "Littergate #6 Puppy." He was the smallest of all the puppies, barely weighed three pounds, and it looked as if he was the sickliest, but my heart knew it was meant to be.

All the volunteers just looked at me and shook their heads as I carried the little guy around as we were working, and they all smiled and said that I failed my first transport test. Once all the dogs and cats were loaded into the transport vans to head back to New Jersey, a prayer group formed, blessing all the rescuers and their special cargo heading to new lives, including a very small and special passenger that afternoon.

I have been involved in rescue for a very long time, close to 30 years, in fact. They say that the animal lets out a long sigh after being rescued. During the long ride home, my team christened him Cado, which means "Gate" in Japanese. He burrowed so deep into my arms, and as I held him, I heard the sigh that he found his home.

We made it home, and my husband fell in love with him as well, and gave him the nickname of "Little Man," since Yoshi and Bella were a lot bigger than he was at the time. We discovered that he was a very sick little boy. In fact, for the next eight months, we thought we were going to lose him, but we showered him with lots of love and medical attention and he grew stronger each day, and finally, the month after being released from the hospital, he was laying on our bed and he let out another sigh.

Our "Little Man" will turn three years old this December. Cado has become my "soul" dog. He climbed onto my leg and into my arms, but he moved into our family's hearts, and my soul. My wish is that all the puppies, adult dogs and cats can enjoy the same happiness that Cado has been given, as they are all God's creatures.

About MaryBeth Yannessa

MaryBeth Yannessa is Board President of Animal House Project. A dog can communicate unconditional love to a human. They allow people who are complete strangers to embrace them, to cry on their shoulders, without one ounce of judgement. A dog looks at you with compassion and understanding that touches your soul. I have seen people stop and fall to their knees and weep with their arms around their heads. I have witnessed bed-ridden elderly raise their frail bodies just to touch a therapy dog's fur. Their eyes would spark with unabated joy like Christmas morning, all just to touch a dog. People need love and to be accepted for who they are, right now. The love that a dog offers not only embraces but empowers with a sense of belonging.

Through Animal House Project we can celebrate the bond between pet and companion. We help people keep their pets which motivates them to love, to share love and to find hope even when all else looks bleak. We help people understand the bond between themselves and their companion pets.

For more Information visit www.AnimalHouseProject.org.

Cado

"The best things in life are rescued."

Sophie

Sophie was adopted from Dog Town Rescue in Colmar, Pennsylvania. We located Sophie by searching for "Labrador rescue" on Google and read the descriptions of the various dogs. Dog Town Rescue is an official 501(c)(3) not-for-profit organization, a no-kill shelter. Their dogs come from local and distant shelters. Jennifer Joseph began Dog Town Rescue as an extension to her premier doggy daycare and boarding facility, with dogs primarily off leash. It's the ultimate stepping stone for a dog waiting to find its forever home. Adopting a dog from Dog Town Rescue truly saves two lives: the dog you adopt, and the dog that takes its place.

www.DogTownRescue.org

My Friend & Exercise Buddy

As I was growing up, I got a dog who became my confidante and friend. Great dog and many, many happy memories! So when our daughter Olivia was young, we adopted two rescue dogs: a 4-month-old mix, Spot, and an eight-year-old German Shepherd mix, Chica. Both were great dogs. Chica had a heart of gold, walked off leash within a week, and blessed our family with love for almost 3 years. Spot became not only my companion, but also one of Olivia's best friends.

I worked from home, and Spot would remind me, "It's lunchtime!" and "It's walk time!" We all loved walking and playing with Spot. As Olivia was nearing college, Spot at 17, became weaker. We finally accepted that Spot was not going to get better and was in pain. We dug her grave that night together—a somber occasion. The next day, I drove Spot to the vet, where they put her to sleep on the grass outside their facility. We all cried.

On the way home, I picked up Olivia from work at lunchtime. We wrapped Spot in a towel and placed her gently in the grave. We said our goodbye prayers and buried her. Olivia and I both went back to work. After work, Dad helped finish burying her (more prayers). My dreams for the next several days were filled with happy memories of Spot, who appeared to be nudging me to get another dog. Another dog needed us.

Olivia would be going off to college within a month, and my husband, Wally, had a heavy travel schedule. I was ready for another dog, but who? I decided to look for an older dog, so the training would be less. I screened the local SPCA sites for a mid to large dog (>40 lbs.) but none caught my eye.

The Labrador rescue site showed several older dogs. I visited several local facilities, searching for the right dog. When I visited Sophie at Dog Town Rescue, she was off leash and calmly greeting the customers and their dogs in the store. The store clerks said that Sophie exercised with other dogs and played well with them. They explained Sophie's circumstances—the new baby in the family had become allergic to dogs, so Sophie went up for adoption. Sophie was six years old, showed a calm temperament, and had our energy level. She interacted well with us at the store. We all agreed, and I adopted Sophie.

As with many adoptions, a few quirks arose. We worked through them by adapting and learning. Sophie enjoyed her new dog bed and participating in obedience training with us. Some days I took her and other days Wally did. We learned a lot there. We, and Sophie, grew together as a team. Watching Cesar Millan (go out the door first) helped us a lot, too. Importantly, I focused on Sophie daily, and did not pester my daughter as she began college. I walked Sophie five times a day when Wally was traveling. Since Wally has retired, they both enjoy walking in the park together. Me, too!

Sophie's normally calm around guests, but one time... as I was walking down the driveway one day, an unfamiliar truck turned up our driveway. Immediately, Sophie (about 90 lbs.) took the middle of the driveway, and barked fiercely several times with a loud, deep, commanding tone. The truck backed up and left. Our neighbor mentioned that burglars had been targeting some of the houses on our street. I am so thankful that our family has Sophie to alert and protect us. Normally, she's her friendly and loving self. Sophie walks easily on the leash, stays near the house off leash, and plays well with kids. Some kids calm down while petting her. Sophie is a terrific dog for us.

In addition. I often need to weave different perspectives together while medical writing, but sometimes I'm not yet satisfied with the section of the document. A walk outside with Sophie relaxes me, improves my health, and often stimulates the needed perspective or new angle. In summary, rescue dogs can bring so much joy to a home for so little cost. It's absolutely worth it.

About Katherine Molnar-Kimber

Kathy Molnar-Kimber, PhD is the scientific consultant and medical writer at KMK Consulting Services of Kimnar Group, LLC. She combines her 20 years as a scientist with her experiences as a peer reviewer, editor, and writer to write posters, scientific and clinical articles for companies, professors in the Life sciences or Medicine, and medical communication companies. She also writes Continuing Medical Education programs for medical education companies, and web pages and blog posts that explain scientific concepts. Kathy volunteers with the American Medical Writers Association - Delaware Valley Chapter as the editor of their newsletter, and as a writer, speaker, and co-chair of a workshop. When not researching and writing, Kathy enjoys walking her dog, gardening (Sophie chases the rabbits), reading, cooking and being with family.

Contact Kathy at kmolnar_kimber@verizon.net.

Kahlua

Kahlua was rescued from the Don't Bully Us Rescue in Philadelphia, PA. Don't Bully Us Rescue is a foster based, Pit Bull and bully breed rescue. They are a non-profit, tax exempt, 501(c)(3) organization whose mission is to rescue, educate, and promote responsible lifetime ownership. Their vision is a society with compassion and kindness toward Pit Bull-type dogs. They help build a community without prejudice or breed-specific legislation. Don't Bully Us adopted dogs are in foster homes throughout the NJ and Philadelphia area, and are saving lives every day with your help.

www.DontBullyUs.com

Every Little Girl Needs a Dog Best Friend

Ever since I was a little girl, I dreamed of having my own dog. I begged my parents when I was old enough to take care of one on my own. I even wrote a full essay on why I should have a dog when I was in 11th grade; I worked on it during all the free time I got in school. I even had a teacher read it over and see if it made him want to get me a dog. He said he felt compelled to give me a dog after reading my essay, so after his approval, I showed my dad the essay.

After a few days of begging and showing him dogs on Facebook that were up for adoption, I found a cute little Pit Bull. She was a pint-size Pit Bull, which is what I was looking for. She was super-friendly, and she jumped around when she got happy. I was going to name her Jelly Bean, but unfortunately, she wasn't spayed, and that would have added another $100 to her $200 adoption fee, which was beyond what I could pay. She was also already six months old, and wasn't trained off leash, or even really on leash. She only knew how to sit and lay down. I would've had my hands full with her, and she would never have been able to fit in my life without training. So, my search continued.

Finally, on July 9th, 2017, my dad got a text from "Don't Bully Us" Pit Bull Rescue, who he works closely with. They said they had a puppy who hasn't gotten adopted yet, and she was the last of her litter. Pit Bulls are my all-time favorite breed of dog, if you couldn't tell already. They sent my dad a picture of a beautiful fawn and black Pit Bull with the most amazing grey eyes you'd ever see. He showed me the text, and I was a bit confused at first, but then he explained that we were going to go look at her, and she was going to be my very own puppy.

The minute I saw her I was in love, I knew she was going to be my puppy for the rest of her amazing life with me. I signed all the papers, got her adoption packet, put her new collar on, and we were off, already starting our first adventure together. She didn't have a name for the first few days I had her. She was just "Puppy" or "Girl" until I found the perfect name to fit her perfect personality – Kahlua (yes, like the alcoholic drink).

She's my everything, I wouldn't trade her for the world. Kahlua is pretty much my very spoiled child. She gets the best food, the best toys, the best seats wherever we go, the whole nine yards. She goes everywhere with me, from going to the barn and spending time with her very large four-legged brother (my horse, Roman), to hiking around every cool place I can find, to swimming in lakes, and even plain old dog parks.

She fits into my life perfectly like a lost puzzle piece finally being put in the puzzle, I'll never find another dog like her, and if I do, it'll be a miracle. I will always choose to adopt first whenever I add another fur-baby to the family, and I will always adopt Pit Bulls, I wouldn't want to spend my life with any other breed.

I am so thankful for Don't Bully Us and my dad because without them, I wouldn't have found my best friend. She is an amazing dog and an amazing ambassador for her breed; without her, I wouldn't have been able to convert so many people in my family and even strangers to consider having Pit Bulls as their next dogs. I've helped so many people find their favorite breed by teaching them about Pit Bulls and having them meet Kahlua. People always say dogs are people's best friends, and they are so right!

Adopting from Don't Bully Us Pit Bull Rescue was one of the easiest and nicest times I've ever had adopting a pet. They take care of everything your puppy needs in their beginning life, from the first set of shots to spay/neuter surgery. They make the experience super easy and very fun. They always find the best pups to match each family.

About Amanda White

Amanda is the owner of Squeels On Wheels Mobile Petting Zoo. Having more than 15 years' experience with animals of all types, she makes her business grow and flourish with her knowledge of animals and knowing how to turn education into fun. When not doing parties and events, Amanda can be found having fun with all her pets or exploring the great outdoors with Kahlua (and her other pups) tagging along.

You can contact Amanda through Facebook and by email at squeelesonwheels@gmail.com.

Zeus

We rescued Zeus from BullyWag in Douglasville, Georgia. They were originally formed in 2008 by a mother/daughter team and became an official Georgia-licensed, non-profit 501(c)(3) animal rescue on July 7, 2009. They started out as strictly a Pit Bull rescue because they were disappointed and frustrated with the huge numbers of Pit Bull-type dogs (or dogs that "look" like Pit Bull-type dogs) being euthanized in the state of Georgia. Their goal was to provide a positive look at Pit Bull-type dogs - promoting and highlighting their outstanding qualities. Today they help rescue all types of needy dogs. They are a volunteer-based rescue that receives no government funding.

www.BullyWagInc.org

Finding the Perfect Dog for Our Family

We wanted to find a perfect dog for our family last year. So, Mom and Dad set some rules because our mom was very clear that there are too many dogs out there that need homes, and told us that we need to rescue one. Our dad said the best dogs he ever had in his life were the ones he rescued, and thanks to our parents' advice, we found the perfect dog for our family, our buddy Zeus.

Our mom and dad said when adopting a dog, you should look for one that is an ideal match for you. No amount of preparation, though, can limit your dog to the characteristics, temperaments, and behaviors that are ideal for you. Nevertheless, thinking through what you want and expect will create a happier outcome. Adopt the perfect dog using the following criteria:

The Dog's Breed and Age

The dog's breed can give you valuable insight into what to expect from a dog. Sure, the breed's temperament and characteristics are just approximations of how the dog could turn out when it's full-grown, and individual dogs have individual personalities. Still, the dog's breed can give you an idea of what to expect. Rescuing a mixed breed may give you fewer clear traits, but mixed breeds usually have better health and temperaments than purebreds.

Everyone falls in love with puppies, but if you don't want to learn about crate training, then you should look into an older puppy or adult dog. Some people prefer only dogs that are two years old or older because they are calmer, house-trained and beyond teething. Puppies and their energy are adorable, but what level of energy do you want? Know yourself and consider the age and breed.

The Dog's Function

Not all people who adopt a dog do so only to make them a pet. There are owners who seek to put their dogs to use according to the dog's activity or training. Some are made into therapy dogs, guide dogs and even epilepsy dogs, which obviously all have had special training. Interestingly, many of these were rescues. Some breeds are trained for hunting, herding, etc.

The Dog's Source

There are plenty of places you can go to when looking for a dog ready for adoption. There are the rescue groups, the animal shelters, and local humane societies for dogs. Some rescue groups specialize in particular breeds or other focuses, which should give you an idea of what to expect with the dogs they shelter.

An animal shelter is the way to go when wanting to save a dog's life. Animal shelters don't necessarily keep track of the dog's history, so you can expect surprises as the dog grows old with you. Also, they often accept mixed breed dogs, or mutts who possess unexpected characteristics. If you are not a big fan of surprises, you can look into the selection of dogs rescue groups have.

Rescue groups are, in general, the best sources for dogs ready for adoption. They keep tabs of their dogs' history and the dogs' previous owners. So, if you are interested in knowing the conditions from wherever the dog you are planning to adopt came from, a rescue group is the best place for you to begin your search. They often foster their dogs in actual homes, not in kennels.

Your Home

Where the dog is going to is also a crucial factor when adopting. Some dog breeds are not suitable for families with children, others are not comfortable in confined places etc.

If you have kids in the family, the size and activities of the dog you are planning to adopt should be considered. Small dogs are likely to be abused when kids are around because often, kids treat their dogs like they would their toys. Very huge dogs, on the other hand, are a big no-no for small kids. Children could be hurt around powerful, muscular, and oversized dogs.

Also check into the policies of your neighborhood and your city. If you are living in an apartment, check with your apartment owner for their pet regulations. You don't want to adopt the perfect dog only to give it back to the shelter because of your living area's no-pet clause policy.

If you use these guidelines like we did, I am sure you will find a wonderful addition to your family like our Zeus is for our family!

About Madison & Brian Bacak

Madison and Brian are two amazing kids who love animals, all types of animals, except snakes! In fact, Madison has her own pet-sitting business and is always booked up every summer. Their parents, who helped write this, are Matt and Stephanie Bacak. Matt is considered by many a digital marketing legend, and Stephanie specializes in helping families that do not qualify for financial aid to pay for college. If you need help easing the college planning pain by making the most of your child's school selection, their financial aid, tax opportunities, and your own savings visit www.CapStoneGlobalAdvisors.com.

Willy

Les Anges Gardiens Des Animaux is located in the Outaouais region of Quebec, Canada and has a very "simple" foundation... the love and respect for animals, especially those who are neglected, abandoned, or abused. It all started about 6 years ago when Johanne Matte's family began collecting funds for the SPCA and started following animal groups on Facebook. They soon met people who had the same interests and slowly started helping animals in need. Since then, they have rescued over 1,000 needy animals. They rescue, socialize, provide veterinary and health care, vaccinate and sterilize animals before finding them a forever home. They also build partnerships with different professionals and organizations to help them fulfill their mission.

www.LesAngesGardiensDesAnimaux.com

Willy Trades in His Treadmill

My day started probably much like most of our days start... browsing my Facebook feed. I wasn't looking for anything, but one comment from a local friend really jumped out at me: "URGENT HELP NEEDED".

The "help" that was being requested was an urgent foster for a two-year-old Labradane that was apparently scheduled for euthanasia on Wednesday.

This was Monday!

Apparently, a family was moving out of the area, and instead of working to find a home for "Willy", the plan was to have him put down. The SPCA had been contacted, but since Willy was deemed an "aggressive" dog that didn't get along well with other animals or people, the only recourse they had was to put him to sleep.

So I didn't hesitate, and I messaged my friend. Two hours later I was in my truck on my way to pick up Willy. I already had two dogs at home, Jazzy and Fred, and I had long ago proclaimed that Border Collies were the only dogs I would ever own. My plan was to foster Willy, rehabilitate him, and then find him his forever home. Every dog I have ever met loved me from our first contact, and I didn't expect things would be any different with Willy.

Boy, was I wrong! The owner brought Willy outside on a leash for us to meet and it took all her strength to hold him back. His hackles were fully raised. He barked. He growled. He lunged... if I didn't know better, I would have thought he wanted to rip my throat out.

But I could see in his eyes; he wasn't aggressive. He was scared. So, I ignored him and his shenanigans while I spoke to his owner. I didn't make eye contact with him. I sat down on the curb. I did everything I could to make myself as non-confrontational as possible.

But after 45 minutes, Willy's stance hadn't changed. He continued to bark, growl and lunge. The owner clearly had no rapport with the animal and was at loss for what to do.

I had hoped that Willy would eventually become curious and come to me on his own accord, but that pipedream was clearly not in the cards. So, I gathered up my courage and asked the owner to hand me the lead, and just as I had suspected, once Willy was in "attack range", he did just the opposite. He did everything he could to run from me and get away. He was terrified. He was NOT vicious.

I simply spoke quietly to him, asking him if he wanted to go for a walk. I thought all dogs knew the words "go for a walk", but apparently Willy hadn't been for many walks. The owner said she couldn't take him on walks because he pulled and was too strong for her. So instead of going outside for walks, Willy was tied onto a treadmill and exercised there instead. Apparently, he loved it!

So for the next hour, Willy and I walked up and down the road in front of his house. And yes, he certainly liked to pull and had no idea what "heel" meant!

But after that hour, Willy no longer feared me. He let me pet him and he nuzzled his nose into my leg. I opened the truck door and before I could even ask him, he jumped in, smiling ear-to-ear. We drove away, and watching him in my rear-view mirror, I noticed he never looked back.

We locked eyes at the first stop sign, and a thought bulleted into my brain: "Prince, is that you?"

Prince was my childhood Yellow Lab and my very best friend growing up. I hadn't read or even heard about "A Dog's Purpose" yet, so you can imagine my excitement when I finally did read the book to learn that Willy could very well be Prince returning to me.

Once home, I introduced Willy to Fred and Jazz. He was initially terrified of these two dogs half his size, but they eventually all made peace, and we headed into the woods for a walk. It was only our first day, but seeing Willy run through the trees, off leash and "off treadmill", literally grinning from ear-to-ear, made me realize that Willy had found his home.

I wasn't fostering him, and he wasn't going anywhere. Since then, Willy has served as my "white shadow". I can't go anywhere or turn around without Willy being right there at my feet.

But the thing is, as much as he thinks he needs me, I need him more. Last October, I experienced the biggest emotional trauma of my life. Willy and I slept in the same bed together and his support helped me survive that first night.

Since my "failed foster" with Willy, we have since successfully fostered and rehomed 4 more "urgent help needed" dogs. Our last dog, a Great Pyrenees named Mica, is our most recent failed foster. Some dogs just belong here with us. There's nothing we can do...

There is nothing more rewarding than rescuing and fostering these amazing, furry, four-legged friends. The time may not seem "right" now, but trust me, if things don't seem "right" now, they will after you bring a rescue into your life.

About Mike Caldwell

Mike Caldwell, a.k.a. "The Marketing Medic", began building sales funnels in 2014. Like many online marketers, Mike initially believed the hype that the tools and the tactics are responsible for your success. But after a couple of years, Mike looked back over both his successful and unsuccessful funnels and realized that although the tools and tactics were the same, the strategies were different. And from that epiphany, the Empathic Market Strategy (EMS) was born. The best way to communicate with your audience is in a way they can relate and respond to. Nothing does that better than showing some empathy. For more information on the Marketing Medic and EMS, please visit www.MarketingMedic.ca.

When not helping entrepreneurs and small businesses with their marketing strategy, Mike lives with his wife Monique and their 4 dogs, 3 horses, 2 pygmy goats and two (rescue) cats in their off-grid home on 164 acres of Gatineau Hills forest.

You can contact Mike by email at mike@mikecaldwell.info.

Fred, Mica & Willy

"The only thing better than one rescue dog is three."

Minnie

It was a video that inspired me to volunteer as a dog walker (and dog runner and dog wrestler) and probably subconsciously inspired me to adopt Minnie. The video "Blind Dog Rescue: Fiona," created by Hope for Paws, tells the story of a terrified little blind dog who was found in squalid conditions in South Los Angeles. Hope for Paws, founded by Eldad Hagar, is a 501(c)(3) non-profit animal rescue organization that rescues dogs, cats and other types of animals suffering on the streets, or were neglected in the wild. Hope for Paw's YouTube channel is filled with heart-warming videos and has over 3 million subscribers. Blind Dog Rescue: Fiona is also a great example of how to use storytelling to inspire people to take action.

www.HopeForPaws.org

12

Blindsided

Who Is This Poor Little Dog?

Walking along the row of cages at the animal shelter where I volunteered, I came to a small, rotund brown and tan Miniature Pinscher-mix running in circles. Her nose pointed almost straight up in the air. She had one under-sized, cloudy eye and one huge, bulging eye, which I subsequently discovered was due to glaucoma, and was later removed.

"What is wrong with this poor little dog?" I thought to myself. What I saw was heartbreaking. She was racing frantically around her cage, stumbling over toys and her bed. She waved her head back and forth, like I had seen blind singers do on TV. The information sheet on the front of her pen included the directive:

"DO NOT VACCINATE. TOO STRESSED OUT."

Between her frantic, clumsy movements and the note, I assumed her behavior was simply due to extreme anxiety. Here she was, a small dog in an unfamiliar place being battered by the non-stop, thunderous barking from two bloodhounds a few cages over, combined with the scent of countless dogs, past and present.

Later, I learned that her head waving and stumbling was because she was blind, and that this little dog, named Minnie by shelter employees, had been found wandering the streets of a small town in southern Maine.

Imagine how scared she must have felt, being blind and left to fend for herself, and then winding up in a strange place. Imagine how vulnerable she must have felt amidst an overpowering mix of peculiar smells and deafening sounds.

No Visitors. No Interest. No Hope of Being Adopted

Minnie remained at the shelter for months. No one came to see her. No one showed any interest in her. As a "special needs dog" with a protruding eye and hugely overweight body, Minnie just couldn't compete with all the cute puppies.

She Deserves a Break…If Only for a Week

Feeling sorry for Minnie, I decided to give her a break from the shelter and take her home for the week the shelter closed to the public during Christmas. When the week was up, I would bring her back.

The moment I put her in the passenger seat, I could sense I might be in trouble.

Agitated and continually distracted moments before at the shelter, Minnie instantly settled in with a sigh, as if she were thinking, "Ah…finally…I'm going home."

A Brand New Dog

Within one day, she was a different dog. She looked happy and relaxed. She started to nuzzle my hand and show interest in being petted. It was only then that I realized how depressed and anxious she had been all that time at the shelter.

The "Week" Without End

When her week was up, I decided I could not, in good conscience, bring her back to a situation that was so hard for her. I asked the shelter manager if we could make her a "by appointment only" dog, where I would house her, and potential owners would set up a time to see her. The shelter manager was, of course, fine with that idea.

Remaining Resolute: "No adoption for me"

Friends and shelter workers would joke with me, saying in a playful singsong voice, "Ohhh...you're going to adopt her!" I would assure them, with complete confidence, that I would NOT be adopting Minnie, because my schedule, including travel, would not allow me to have a dog. I would continue to get my "dog fix" by volunteering.

Caving-In

This lasted for about two months, when it became clear to me that I could never give up this amazing little dog. She had totally wriggled her way into my heart. So, on February 10th, 2014, I officially adopted Minnie, who I now call "The Min Pin."

The Gift That Blindsided Me

As I reflect on our four-plus years together, I find it amusing to think back on how I thought I was doing HER a favor by adopting her. When I adopted The Min Pin, my life felt full and fulfilling. I wasn't looking for something else to bring me joy or fill up any emptiness.

Yet...I can totally relate to the bumper stickers I see on cars that say Who Rescued Whom? when I think about the laughter, joy, and love this wacky little dog has brought into my life.

When she wakes up each morning, she wriggles and squirms with delight as she gets her first dose of adoration, mixed with ear and neck scratches. When it's time to eat, she leaps up in the air and dances around on her hind legs like a miniature Lipizzaner stallion. Besides having the classic Min Pin quirkiness, which makes me and those who know her laugh, she is also an unassuming source of inspiration.

My "MinPinspiration"

Her blindness doesn't slow her down a bit. In fact, I often forget she's blind because of her "go for it" attitude. If she does run into something, most of the time she doesn't even shake her head; she merely careens off the object without missing a beat. When I let The Min Pin free range at the beach, she will sprint full tilt, with zero hesitation.

For all the love and joy this wacky little dog brings to my life, perhaps the biggest impact is the lesson she embodies each day... "It's not what happens to you, it's what you DO with it that matters."

About David Lee

David Lee is the founder of the consulting firm Human-Nature@Work (HumanNatureAtWork.com) where he focuses on helping organizations cultivate a resilient, high-performing work-force. He has also been involved in using and teaching storytelling for counseling, coaching, leadership communication, and marketing for over 25 years. His website, which is devoted to storytelling, is www.StoriesThatChange.com and he can be reached at david@humannatureatwork.com.

DAVID LEE

Minnie & David

"Be the person your dog thinks you are."

Napa

Napa was rescued at the Best Friends Animal Society in Kanab, Utah. In 1984, the founders of Best Friends made a promise to one another and to the animals already in their care that they would build an animal sanctuary in Southern Utah, where they could dedicate their lives to housing and finding homes for un-wanted pets while advocating the importance of no kill. Over 30 years later, they have inspired others throughout the country to take up the mantle of no kill and have helped to reduce the number of animals being killed in shelters by 91 percent.

www.BestFriends.org

When They Say, "Who Rescued Who?" They're Not Kidding

My mom is a big animal person and wanted me to volunteer at Best Friends Animal Society in Kanab, Utah. Kanab is in the middle of nowhere and I had no desire to go there, and no thought of adopting. But I went to make my mom happy, and I'm so glad I did.

While I was volunteering at Best Friends, I saw this dog in a pen by himself, and he just caught my eye. I think he caught my eye because he was all black, in a shaded pen, and all I could see was his teeth opening and closing as he breathed. For some reason I just kept looking at him. He was tall, long-legged and dark as midnight.

I asked the staff why he was alone, and they said he'd just come in and needed to be evaluated. I volunteered to take him for an overnight evaluation and brought him to the hotel where my mom, a friend and her three kids were staying.

As soon as we got in the room I knew this dog was different. I said, "Jump on the bed!" and he started jumping from bed to bed in the hotel. The kids and I were howling with laughter.

We finally stopped the bed jumping, and then the dog did the most interesting thing...one of the kids has cerebral palsy and must use a walker. She gets tired easily and was sitting in a chair. The dog, who just finished jumping on the beds, backed up to her chair and literally sat on her lap, while keeping all four feet on the floor.

The look on this little girl's face was indescribable - here she is struggling and a bit isolated in life, and this dog chooses her to just literally, well, sit on! The girl had huge eyes, mouth agape and a face flushed with love – it was like the little girl was feeling chosen and wanted and loved.

I wound up falling in love with that dog... but adopting just didn't make sense. I was just coming out of a rough time, and finances were tight. Real tight. But this dog just felt right, and I put in to adopt him. I remember I didn't care about making money for myself, but I needed to make money to adopt and then take care of him.

The day I was going to adopt him, I just had enough cash to buy gas to get to Kanab to pick him up, but I didn't have enough to get home. Somehow it worked out, I got him and got home, and my finances have never been as tight as they were that day.

I could tell you countless stories of how he's brightened my life and that of others, and I'll just tell this one to wrap up: how he brightens my morning.

When we wake up, Napa is happy to see me. He's just happy, like he's happy to have another day and start it with someone he loves. Usually I hate mornings. When I see him so happy, I think to myself, "If he's that happy, there's no reason I can't be," and I get happy, too.

Napa has brought joy, love, new friends and a healthier lifestyle to me and my life...and I hope you find a dog that does the same for you! Napa pulled me the rest of the way out of the pit I'd been in, and he keeps helping make it better.

Final thought... Napa's made me a better man. He's a pretty special pup, and people love to meet him. They love it so much, in fact, that I think about how he touches lives, and how I want to do the same. Seeing how a dog is blind to preconceptions about people based on looks, demographics or standing in society makes me want to love people the way he does.

About Jase Souder

Jase is the creator of the Profitable Presentations training series, where business owners learn how to effectively use public speaking to grow their businesses. Profitable Presentations allow businesses to "Make a Difference and Make a Lot of Money." Praised as a leader in authentic business, Jase is a nationally recognized speaker and trainer, specializing in personal development, public speaking and sales. He's been published in eight books, appeared in two movies and has appeared on national and local TV and radio.

Learn more about Jase at www.JaseSouder.com.

Emanuel

Emanuel was rescued from the Animal House Shelter in Huntley, Illinois, which is a non-profit, no-kill, 501(c)(3) shelter for all breeds of dogs and cats. They rescue, care for and find homes for homeless pets who arrive at the shelter for various reasons, and could really use some love.

Once the animals are rehabilitated and ready, they are carefully matched with people for adoption or foster care. Their mission is to find loving, stable homes for all of the pets in their care. Over 38,000 pets have found a forever home with the Animal House Shelter since its founding in 2002.

www.AnimalHouseShelter.com

Emanuel – "Dog with Us"

My beautiful wife Michele and I had started talking about getting a doggie soon after we got married and moved into our first home. We never considered getting one from a pet store or breeder, knowing that there are plenty of great doggies living in shelters who need people to make them a part of their family. We knew that we would always remember and appreciate that we had rescued our doggie, and that our doggie would, too.

Only a few months after we had moved into our new home, Michele's birthday was less than a week away when I heard about a local animal shelter that just happened to be named after the greatest movie of all time, National Lampoon's Animal House. I took that as a sure sign that we were about to find the perfect birthday present for Michele.

We knew one great thing about rescuing a doggie from a shelter is that we could connect with one who already had the ideal personality that we wanted. I wanted a doggie who would have tons of energy and would always be ready to run, jump and play. Michele wanted a doggie she could cuddle with. We knew it would be quite a tall order to find both traits in one doggie, but we had faith that we would.

As we waited in a special doggie/family meeting room, I let the shelter volunteers know my simple test: I would toss a tennis ball across the room, and if the doggie ran and got it and brought it back to me, that was our doggie. Michele wanted a doggie to respond to her call and come to her to be petted.

The volunteers listened to our wants and went to find our perfect doggie – cautioning us that they might not be able to fulfill all our desires. We were prepared to leave disappointed, but I reminded everyone that this was the Animal House Shelter, so I knew in my heart that our ideal doggie must be there.

The first doggie came into the room and was very nice, but when I threw the ball, he or she just sat there and looked at it. Next!

Doggie #2 ran and picked up the ball when I threw it, but then just sat there and kept it. Strike two.

Then our doggie entered the room. But he didn't just enter the room – he burst onto the scene and completely took it over.

Several other families were seated around the outside of the room, leaving a wide-open space in the middle. A few doggies were visiting with people, hoping to find new homes. Suddenly, our doggie ran full speed into the room, and made a few full-speed laps around the middle area. Tons of excitement and energy? Check.

When we called and motioned the rambunctious cocker spaniel to stop and say hello to us, he jumped right up onto the couch next to Michele and nestled into her as she petted him. Responsive and affectionate? Check. Everything looked good so far.

Then came the moment of truth. The shelter volunteers held their breath, hoping this one passed my test. I tossed the ball across the room. Our doggie immediately ran full speed to it, picked it up, and ran back to me with it. He did it over and over, in fact, and didn't want to stop.

Sound the trumpets! We had a winner! As soon as we got home and opened the door, our new family member ran in and repeated his full-speed lap-running routine from room to room, so overwhelmingly excited to be out of his cage and inside his new home. (*He would repeat this routine every time one of us came home – even if I just went 20 feet to take out the garbage. What a great doggie!)

We named him Emanuel, which means "God with us" in Hebrew. He was our "Dog with us," and for the next 13 years he taught us every moment of every day about unconditional love and support. The feeling was, of course, mutual. No matter what happened in our lives, Michele and I always knew that we had love in our home and in our lives. Emanuel never cared about the past or the future – he just loved us in every moment and brought us non-stop joy.

Emanuel left this Earth about two years ago – but he will never leave our hearts.

About Steve Sipress

Steve Sipress is recognized as one of the most-requested, in-demand small business sales and marketing consultants in the world. He is a successful serial entrepreneur, who has created and built over a dozen successful companies of his own, while helping thousands of other ambitious and aggressive business owners and entrepreneurs all around the world do the same over the past 35+ years. Steve has assembled a team of the world's top business-building experts as the publisher of Rhino Monthly Magazine, the Rhino Daily Blog and the Rhino Daily Podcast.

He has written numerous newsletters and articles on sales and marketing for a wide range of publications, has appeared on radio, television and in international media, and is the best-selling author of over 20 books. Steve is the behind-the-scenes, go-to marketing advisor for many top business owners and entrepreneurs in all 50 states and 26 countries worldwide, in 165+ different industries.

Connect with Steve on Facebook or at www.SteveSipress.com.

Calvin

The Homeless Pet Foundation, located in Marietta, Georgia, was founded by Dr. Michael Good, owner of the Town and Country Veterinary Clinic, to prevent unnecessary euthanasia and to find an alternative solution for the many lost dogs and cats in our community that are in overcrowded shelters. This organization is run 100% by volunteers, dedicated to promoting responsible pet ownership while placing adoptable dogs and cats in forever homes. The common goal is to save the lives of homeless pets. The adoption site is open Monday through Saturday at Town and Country Veterinary Clinic, 1343 Gresham Road, Marietta, GA 30062 from 8:00am-6:00pm. There is also a weekend adoption site at PetSmart on Johnson Ferry Road in Marietta where I adopted my dog, Calvin.

www.HomelessPets.com

That Happy Expressive Face

It was Saturday, December 8, 2012, and I was on a frenetic mission running around town gathering Christmas gifts for all my friends and family. My daughter, her husband and three children were arriving the following weekend from California, so all the decorations needed to be up, and gifts wrapped and hidden. On my Saturday list was pellets for my African Grey parrot, Quincy, and after my flight through both double doors at PetSmart, my brain registered a really cute face of a dog in the first cage of the weekend adoption. I turned around, went back outside, looked into his eyes and asked if the volunteer would let him out. We spent about ten minutes together and I said, "I'll take him if I can come back at 3:00 to pick him up."

Yes, that may have seemed impulsive, but I felt an immediate connection. I had just spent the last 8 months nursing a Golden Retriever mix rescue who I had adopted, and five years later he suddenly developed stomach cancer. His suffering was devastating. I was emotionally spent, but there was something about the intellectual and happy expression of that dog in the cage that reignited my heart. It was an instantaneous connection for both of us.

From that day in December, Calvin has been my shadow; or maybe, it's vice versa. We are inseparable. He reads my mind almost before my thought processes. He definitely understands and responds to my movements, and I'm certain he can tell time, as I receive a consistent reminder for meals, walks, and our together time by his alert ears, wagging tail and enthusiastic expression.

I'm a realtor in North Metro Atlanta, and Calvin came to work with me each day. The brokerage that my son and I owned was on the second floor of an office building. Calvin was initially terrified of both cars and stairs so I always carried sandwich bags of treats, and after much coaxing and a trail to follow, we managed to overcome his fears and gain his trust. He did enjoy a big comfy bed and new visitors to our office, and it soon became his second home. He also loved our walks through the office complex where he met other dogs, as well as many new friends. We were together the greater part of each day and I loved it. My current broker, Atlanta Fine Homes Sotheby's International Realty, with which we are now associated, also features a comfy dog bed in their lobby for any four-legged friends along with their beautiful designer furnishings for all agents, clients and pet owners.

Calvin is calm, loving and speaks with his facial expressions, along with his alert ears and ever-wagging tail; but most certainly, he speaks with his heart. We are so in tune with each other that words are often unnecessary. His love and loyalty go well beyond anything I could have imagined in an adopted dog. We are truly soulmates and thankful we have each other.

My family raised retrievers outside of Cleveland, Ohio when I was a child. My grandfather, his brother and my father all served at Presidents of the Buckeye Retriever Club. My dad was frequently asked to be a judge at the Ohio Trials as well as the National Trials. A dog that I trained as a child went on to participate in the National Trials, so I was always surrounded by high-performing and well-bred dogs. Yet the bond that Calvin and I have was never this present with any other dog.

All that being said, why is this adopted dog, mostly black Lab with, perhaps, a hint of Shar-Pei, the love of my life? I will never know where Calvin came from, but he has several "survival" scars, and even a bullet pellet in his neck, presumably, from when he was on the run. None of my vets recommend removing it, and it certainly is not hurting him in any way. I imagine he was foraging for food in someone's garbage can or chicken coop. He was frightened and skinny when I adopted him, but now is calm, loving, aware of and attentive to every move I make, and communicates through his amazing happy expressions and ever wagging tail. Our bond is as deep as it is broad.

Every afternoon at about 5:30, Calvin appears with his ears perked and tail wagging as he gives me a gentle nudge that it is time for our walk, which is a very special time for just the two of us to get out in the neighborhood and do our mile walk where we share ideas, thoughts and just listen to each other. It's been our routine ever since he arrived in my life, and one we both look forward to each day. I carry on a philosophical conversation regarding the world events, or just my daily happenings, and he listens to every word with an alert and compassionate expression until a squirrel or other four-legged creature crosses our path, where we have a momentary diversion before resuming our evening walk.

The miracle of Calvin began on that hurried December day, and we have relished in each other's friendship ever since, and I anticipate many more years of friendship, joy, and companionship. When you pass the adoption centers and look into the eyes of the amazing opportunities of a lifetime of companionship, take time to stop and understand that one of those wonderful souls with bright eyes and a wagging tail would love to become part of your life. It's up to you to make it happen, and not for a single moment will you ever be happier that you gave this wonderful dog a home and a life for you both to cherish together.

About Lynn Horner Baker

Lynn Horner Baker is a professional Realtor with Atlanta Fine Homes Sotheby's International Realty in the North Metro Atlanta area. An active and prominent Realtor since 1991, Lynn's service covers all of Cobb County, South Cherokee County and North Fulton County. Additionally, Lynn's credentials include being a Certified Luxury Home Specialist, a Master Certified Negotiation Expert as well as an Accredited Home Stager with a degree in Interior Design, all of which help her clients better buy and/or sell their homes with the confidence that they will receive the best possible results.

You can reach Lynn at lynn@hornerbakerpartners.com or www.HornerBakerPartners.com.

Calvin

"Rescued is my favorite breed."

Gizmo

Berks Animal Rescue League, located in Birdsboro, Pennsylvania, is where we have adopted four pets, including Gizmo and fostered two other pets from. Berks ARL is now a no-kill shelter, having just moved to that status in the last 12 months. They have 10,000+ animals move through their facility each year. The Berks ARL is active in the community, offering spay/neuter and shot clinics, fun events to get their fosters out into the public space, and even bringing pets to retirement homes for socialization. They are a 501(c)(3) organization and would welcome any support you may be able to offer them because of reading this chapter.

www.BerksARL.org

Everyone Deserves at Least One Great Dog

I am a firm believer that wealth is not just a monetary aspect of life. There are many ways to be wealthy. True, that monetary wealth and freedom can fund a lot of other wealth -based endeavors. However, whether rich or poor, we all can help one another in this world. We can all help those with less of an advantage in life than we have had, and we should help those who cannot help themselves, including animals and pets.

It is this belief that has lead our family to be active with our local animal rescue, and to be a foster family, as well.

Over the years, and previously as individuals, we have had a handful of rescue dogs. Our first rescue dog as a family was Sidney Vicious – "Sid" for short, and "vicious" for her poor kennel behavior – and all she needed was a chance. She was a grumpy mix of Chihuahua and Dachshund, with an underbite of nearly an inch, and a curly tail almost 12" in length - she wasn't winning any awards anytime soon. She was a happy dog, though, and loved walks. She was also quite cunning, able to escape our fenced-in backyard on numerous occasions. Despite always having about ten pounds too many on her oddly shaped frame, she was able to scale our fence in a certain low spot that afforded her the ability to lift her plump body over the fence line. She would escape and return to the front door, she never did figure out how to get back over the fence!

There was also Blue Dog, a rather large Black Lab who was overfed table food all his life and had little to no opportunity for exercise, kept in a hoarding situation with little human interaction. We brought him home at 145 pounds! He had a happy life with us, but never quite bonded with our family the way we had hoped, but still we were happy to be his family and him be our Blue Dog for about 5 years till he finally passed on.

Then there is Gizmo. Gizmo is my boy. He is both my dog and our family dog. But he is my dog. I forget exactly how we came up with his name. But I remember the day we all decided to bring him home. There were plenty of other cuter dogs; "safer" dogs; dogs without the baggage that is attached to Pit Bull breed. In the end, we took a chance and brought Gizmo home. I will tell you this much; never have we had a more loving, more affectionate, more active participant in our family than with Gizmo. He is truly an amazing dog. It's said you get one great dog in life. If this is true, I am elated, as we have many more years ahead together with our boy Gizmo.

I've included a photo of the day we brought Gizmo home, taken within his first hour with us in our home. It's a bit out-of-focus, but it captured the happiness he immediately brought to our family. My sons are smiling and so is Gizmo! For weeks on end he wouldn't leave our side. He was with someone every waking moment for those first weeks. Just in range as though to say, "I'm here for you if you need me, and I love being a part of this family."

If you've never considered rescuing a dog, I cannot say it with anymore emphasis than: "Just do it!" The love and appreciation given by a rescued dog is indescribable, and you and your family will never be the same.

About Jeff Giagnocavo

Jeff Giagnocavo is a co-owner of Gardner's Mattress & More in Lancaster, PA. For nearly 30 years, Gardner's has been helping their community wake up happy each morning. Gardner's also supports their community by collecting food donations with each mattress delivery they make as well as donating monthly to various charities including animal rescue organizations.

Visit www.GardnersMattressAndMore.com.

Gizmo

"Happiness starts with a wet nose and ends with a tail."

Dodie

Animal Friends of the Valleys (AFV), located in Wildomar, California, is dedicated to promoting humane care of animals through education and a humane, pro-active animal services program. They are committed to preventing the suffering of animals and to ending pet overpopulation in the communities they serve.

AFV's vision is to be recognized as the leading shelter by providing a safe haven for all animals, while becoming a full service animal care facility that offers quality and affordable care. Through community education and involvement, AFV will reach their vision to end pet overpopulation and find a home for every adoptable pet in their shelter.

www.AnimalFriendsOfTheValleys.com

Dodie Maronie – the Best Dog Ever !

I've owned a few dogs in the last 35 years, and every one of them were near and dear to me. I love dogs unconditionally, and they really are a man's best friend.

Currently, I have nine small dogs living with me, and my goal is to have a refuge where anyone can bring their lost strays. All dogs deserve love, a warm, caring home, someone that cares about them, and the best food money can buy. By the way, all these nine dogs have a condo inside my home. Not directly inside the main area of my home, but a bed/condo right inside the back door.

To be honest, they don't run around in my home unattended and free. They don't care about doing that, but they do, however, have a big yard to run and play in while protected from the elements and other larger, predatory animals. If you let your dogs run free without a fence, you're risking an accident with a car, and therefore I never allow them in the front yard unless they have their leash on for a walk.

Dodie Maronie was one of my most interesting rescues. She apparently was either lost or dumped on the side of the road by someone three or four days before I found her and rescued her. This one road trip event turned out to be a godsend for me.

12 years ago, I was driving two hours to my office one way daily. That fateful morning, I found Dodie on the side of the road in Oklahoma at about 6 a.m. It was pitch dark, which makes this save even more important.

I didn't notice this initially, but she was covered with ticks. Not a lot them, but enough of them that had had enough time to suck some blood from her tiny little body (I started working on these ticks as soon as I could. It took me a few weeks to get rid of all those ticks, but it was worth it to me).

She'd apparently been running around in the countryside for at least three or four days (due to the size of the ticks) and I vividly remember that morning.

I was driving my SUV about 65 mph, and luckily, I something moving in front of me on the black asphalt road. Dodie's not a big dog. She weighs around nine pounds, but she could have been run over very easily because it was like driving at midnight.

When I slowed down, I could see that she was a small dog, but I didn't know if someone had just lost her, so I drove by her. My brain immediately went into overload. I said to myself, "Here's a dog that needs to be rescued," so I drove another 1,000 feet, then slammed on the brakes.

I shoved the car in reverse, turned around and drove back as fast as I could. I knew that if I didn't rescue her then and take her, she could be run over, and I'd be to blame, so that wasn't an option. As I drove back, she never ran. She just stood there in the middle of the road.

When I stopped and got out of my SUV, she just rolled over on her back and put her paws up, surrendering to me. She did not yelp or make a single sound.

I picked her up, said a few nice things to her, asked her if she wanted a ride to the next town with me, and then put her on the rider's seat. As soon as I got in and buckled up, she immediately came over to my side, snuggled up close to me, and just sat there staring out the window for the next hour.

When I got to the clinic, I took her inside. I introduced her to the staff, and they loved on her like I did. Since she didn't have a name yet, one of the medical assistants said, "Name her Dodie." I didn't particularly like that name, but the more I said it, the more it fit, so that became her first name.

I gave her a middle name within three days. I called her Maronie, which rhymes with Dodie. She had her first and middle name, so I gave her my last name - Carney. Now it was official. She was mine, and nothing or no one was going to take her away.

She is, without a doubt, a very loyal dog. She sleeps with me, follows me around and is always waiting for me at the front door when I return from my daily errands. When I'm working on marketing projects, she's always at my feet, just like she is now. She'll wait up at night, and never complains. She is my girl, my Alpha dog, and I love her unconditionally, just like she loves me.

About Dr. Ivan Carney

Dr. Ivan Carney is a copywriter, chiropractor, connector, speaker, author of eight books, acupuncturist, visionary, and direct response marketer. He has a wide array of services and skills and has discovered certain items that help people with dementia, Alzheimer's, weight loss, memory loss, and most of all, chronic pain. He's now opening a new practice in Murrieta, CA, The Health Intervention & Pain Relief Center, which will be the Inland Empire's premier pain relief center. This one entity will soon be licensed on a global scale once the marketing is tested, completed and in place.

Rusty

The mission of First Coast No More Homeless Pets, located in Jacksonville, Florida, is to end the killing of shelter cats and dogs in our community, northeast Florida, southeast Georgia, and across the nation. First Coast No More Homeless Pets helps people and their pets with high quality, low-cost veterinary care through our sustainable industry-leading programs, services and solutions. We are not a shelter; we make shelters stronger with a broad range of comprehensive programs like our Pet Food Bank, large-scale adoption events, and through low-cost or no-cost spay neuter programs.

www.FCNMHP.org

From Heartbreak to Happiness

Sometime in the summer of 2000, I heard a whining at our front door. I opened the door and there was this small German Shepherd-looking dog. She cocked her head at me with pointed ears and whined again.

I stepped outside and closed the door behind me. I couldn't let her in because we had cats. I kneeled and petted her, and she was all over me... so affectionate. I brought her into our screened-in porch and got her some water and wet cat food. She gobbled the food down, so I got her another can and watched that disappear, too.

When my wife Nancy came home, she asked me what we were going to do with her. She asked me this while getting affectionately mauled. So, I sort of knew what her intentions were. We lived in a gated community, so she had to belong to someone in the community. She had no collar on. I contacted the gate with the description and posted a sign at the gate. After three days, no one came forward to claim her... which was a mystery.

Where did she come from, and why did she come to our door out of all the doors she passed?

I didn't care - she was ours, and we named her Jenny. We introduced her to our three cats. She loved them, and they tolerated her at first, then grew to love her. In the years we had her, it wasn't unusual to see a cat curled up with her. In 2010, Jenny died with her head in my lap. She had bone cancer. She was the sweetest dog.

Two years later, I asked Nancy if she was ready to get another dog. She wasn't sure. I went to my computer and searched for the local Animal Control, which was a kill shelter. If I was going to get a dog, I was going to go where I could save a dog's life. On their site they had short videos of dogs available for adoption. I started watching the videos.

Jenny used to do this thing I loved; with her head turned away from you, she would cock those beautiful brown eyes at you. I was watching the sixth video, which featured a medium-size brown dog with a white chest and white on the tip of his tail. He wasn't looking at the camera. Then suddenly, without moving his head, he cocked his eyes at me. Well, to be more specific, he cocked his eyes at the camera. I yelled to Nancy, "Get ready, we're going to Animal Control."

I told them about the dog I had seen in the video and asked if he was still available. They said yes and ushered us into a small room that had some dog toys scattered around. He completely ignored Nancy and me. Nothing like Jenny's first reaction to us. Just started playing with the toys.

To be honest, I wasn't that impressed. But I kept remembering the way he had cocked his eyes at me in the video. Well, we decided to give him a try. On the way home, we stopped at PetSmart and picked him up food, a new leash, new food and water bowls, and some toys.

We brought him home, and as soon as we opened the front door, he started terrorizing the cats. Not being mean but chasing them. You could tell he wanted to play with them. They were having none of it.

For the next three months, we had to lock the cats out on the screened porch to keep them separated from him. They weren't happy. We seriously considered taking him back to Animal Control.

After those three months, we let the cats back in, and today I can tell you that every cat not only tolerates him but loves him. They are always following him around, washing him and playing with him.

We named him Rusty. When we took him to the vet, she said he was about 9 months old. He's turned out to be the perfect dog. I've never had a dog like him. All the dogs in the neighborhood like him. There is a German Shepherd across the street that will go through her electronic fence just to play with him.

It's hard for me to believe that if we hadn't adopted him, he would've been put to death. Save a dog's (and cat's) life today. ADOPT!

About Michael Gravette

After serving in the Air Force, including Air Force Intelligence during the Vietnam War, Michael Gravette founded Safety Technology in 1986. Since then, Safety Technology has become the largest drop ship wholesaler of self-defense products, hidden cameras, spy and surveillance systems in the country.

Learn more at www.SafetyTechnology.org.

Bruno

Bruno was rescued from the Baltimore Animal Rescue and Care Shelter (BARCS) in Baltimore, Maryland. BARCS is a non-profit, 501(c)(3) organization, operating Maryland's largest animal shelter and pet adoption center. They are an open-admission shelter, granting refuge to every abandoned, neglected, abused, lost or surrendered animal that comes through their door. Along with animal adoption services, BARCS provides resources and low-cost services to pets and people in the community. Free and low-cost medical vaccine clinics, off-site community days, and our public food bank are just some of the ways they are helping pet owners in need, and touching the lives of thousands of families in their community.

www.BARCS.org

19

Saved from the
Mean Streets of Baltimore

David, my youngest son, had started asking about getting a dog when he was as young as four years old. He didn't realize what a "BIG ASK" this was, since he was growing up in a "cat family." As we began to talk seriously about getting a dog, it was David who insisted we get a rescue dog. At first, I was hesitant to get "someone else's" dog, especially not knowing the dog's history. About two years into our search, we heard about the Baltimore Animal Rescue and Care Shelter (BARCS).

We live about 45 miles away, but we were impressed that BARCS is an open-admission shelter, granting refuge to every abandoned, neglected, abused, lost or surrendered animal that comes through their door. A staggering 30 or more animals are surrendered to BARCS every day. No matter what the circumstance, BARCS does not turn away any animal in need of shelter, food, medical care and a loving touch. Yearly, this equates to more than 11,000 dogs, puppies, cats and kittens.

Growing up in Baltimore City is not easy. Just recently, Baltimore was named the most dangerous city in America. Being a dog on the mean streets of Baltimore can be even tougher. Bruno was brought to BARCS after having been freed from an underground illegal dog fighting operation. A mix between a Doberman and Chocolate Lab, Bruno probably would not have survived the pit, and his rescuers believed he was being raised as a "bait dog."

What immediately impressed us about Bruno is how smart he is; what we fell in love with is how sweet he is. Bruno is half-Doberman and half-Chocolate Lab. I don't think there is a better combination of breeds. He is both "wicked smart" and a gentle giant.

From day one, Bruno has been my running buddy, and helped me to get into a routine of working out 5-6 days a week. In fact, there are days I don't want to get out of the bed, but Bruno knows it's time to work out, and gently nudges me into action.

Bruno totally changed my attitude about rescue animals. Last year I was doing a TV tour to promote my book, and while in Tucson, Arizona, I shared the stage with Marco, a stray cat that was the "Pet of the Week" from a kill shelter in southern Arizona. After a brief conversation with my wife, I brought Marco home from Tucson, and from the moment they first met, he and Bruno have been best buddies. I could not imagine life without Bruno, and now Marco. Rescue dogs (and cats) are the best dogs!

About Sherman Ragland

Sherman Ragland, CCIM, helps people interested in getting into real estate to get their very first deal in as little as 21 days. ABC - TV Has named him "America's Real Estate Mentor." He is the Dean of the Realinvestors® Academy and the Realinvestors' Online University, REIU. He is the Host of Real Investors™ Talk Radio.com, a program dedicated to assisting people in all walks of life to learn the correct way to invest in real estate. Sherman is also the Founder of DC-REIA.COM, the Greater Washington, DC Real Estate Investors' Association (www.dcreia.com), the largest and most successful real estate training organization in the DC, Northern Virginia and Central Maryland region.

To learn more, visit www.ShermanRagland.com.

Bruno

"Rescued dogs are super!"

Cartwright

North Shore Animal League America, located in Port Washington, New York, is a pioneer in the no-kill movement, implementing a no-kill policy to ensure that the animals they rescue receive the care and support they need. It is the largest animal rescue and adoption organization in the world, serving the New York City area and across the country, and has saved more than 1,000,000 lives.

www.AnimalLeague.org

A Bonanza of Love

The Verrazano Bridge was closed for the New York City Marathon. We lived on Long Island and were planning to visit Maryann's mom in Staten Island, and with the bridge closed, we had a Sunday afternoon unexpectedly free.

We had just bought a house. As long-time residents of New York City, we wanted a dog to call our own, but the building we lived in prohibited it. As homeowners, we could now enlarge our family by one.

North Shore Animal League is the world's largest no-kill shelter. Maryann's childhood dog, Randy, had been brought home by her brother, John, from North Shore when he was a little puppy. Randy had been an amazing dog, so naturally, we went right to North Shore.

We knew that we wanted a girl and a medium-sized breed. A nice, calm dog would be wonderful, of course. We walked through the facility and looked at all sorts of beautiful dogs. There was one little girl at the end of the first row who sat quietly while her kennel mate lost his mind.

She would be ours.

We asked to play with her and quickly fell in love. As we looked her over, we noticed something.

He would be ours.

Someone had put the wrong card on his kennel. So, we wouldn't be adopting a girl after all. But we never considered not taking him home.

Once we were home, we looked at his paws. This wasn't a medium-sized dog at all. He was already 45 pounds at six months of age. We didn't realize he'd grow into the 90-pound bundle of love he is today.

As we debated names, we thought about naming him 'Hoss' for the bigger brother on Bonanza, but we were both 'Little Joe' fans growing up, and this handsome boy wouldn't be little for long.

What to do?

Cartwright. The family name. Because all the Cartwright boys were good men, and we wanted our Cartwright to be a good doggy.

And so, Cartwright joined our family. He was our baby, and he knew it.

When we added a real human child to the family, we were concerned. Would Cartwright love her? Accept her? Would he feel left out? Our daughter, like our son, was adopted. So, it wasn't like Cartwright was able to go through the pregnancy with us and understand what was happening in that manner.

Cartwright was our firstborn. We knew that we had to manage the transition in the best way possible, so that our family would be complete and happy and whole. We never once considered giving him up.

During Keagan's first week home, we kept the two separate, meeting only at a gate. We brought her blankets out for Cartwright to sleep on, to get used to her scent. We focused lots of attention on him so that he did not feel displaced.

On the first night we all spent in the family room watching television, he went over to his little sister, sniffed her gently, kissed her nose and settled down beside us.

But it wasn't until we took Keagan to her crib that we knew he would love and protect her like he did us. We had accidentally left her little blanket on the couch. When Maryann turned back to get it, we saw Cartwright hurrying after us from the family room, blanket in mouth. He brought it to her proudly. She was his, like we were.

Cartwright is now a sturdy eleven-year-old. He's a big brother to two human siblings and two canine ones. The littlest is a puppy adopted from North Shore in February of this year. It's been fun watching Cartwright take on the role of "Big Daddy" to his little canine sister, teaching her all his most important tasks:

- Always greet your people happily.
- Always give them kisses when they need it – whether they know it or not.
- Always ask – somewhat politely – for whatever food they are eating.
- Always love and protect them.

Cartwright is the best dog we could ever hope for or ask for – even though we went looking for a medium-sized girl puppy, this big, goofy, happy, loud, sweet, sensitive boy makes our house a home, and we hope he lives forever. No matter what, he will in our hearts.

About Francine E. Love

Francine E. Love is the Founder and Managing Attorney of LOVE LAW FIRM, PLLC, a New York-based law firm dedicated to meeting the needs of businesses and entrepreneurs. After a lifetime on Wall Street, she opened her own firm to make C-suite legal services available and cost-effective for Main Street businesses.

It is Francine's desire that LOVE LAW FIRM, PLLC be known as a different type of law firm. As she shares, "If other lawyers are considered sharks, LOVE LAW FIRM, PLLC are the dolphins. Only a daring few people pay for 'shark experiences' where they defy death while being suspended in an underwater cage and are attacked. But one of the most popular attractions in warmer climates for people of all ages is the 'swimming with the dolphins' encounter. Hiring a lawyer shouldn't feel like a near-death experience."

To reach Francine, call 516-697-4828 or visit her website at www.LoveLawFirmPLLC.com.

Sophie

Searching for another Yellow Lab lead us to the Lake Erie Labrador Retriever Rescue, Inc. (LELRR) based in Bath, Ohio. They've been a 501(c)(3) organization since 1999, serving the needs of Labrador Retrievers without human families in northeast Ohio and western Pennsylvania. Their care about the care-giver their adopted dogs will live with is outstanding. Learn more at:

www.LELRR.org

LELRR posted a dog, Autumn (who became Sophie), from Lawrence County Humane Society in New Castle, PA., who we fell in love with. Since 1953 they've focused on preventing cruelty to animals. Their caution for the other dogs their adopted dogs will live with is outstanding. Learn more at:

www.LawrenceCountyHumane.com

Sophie's Well-Deserved Crown

"I've seen this Lab (Autumn)...she is very happy,
loves people, good with other dogs
(could care less about them, only wanted my attention.)"

Those words from the Lab rescue group captured our attention, but it was her picture that grabbed our hearts. My wife Teresa and I, separately, saw her picture one morning, but hesitated to tell one another, because we both 'knew' this was our dog—simply by looking at her picture.

Then the tingles came. The special tingles you get when you know something is right. I couldn't stop staring at her picture. I sensed her character through her goofy look, along with her tongue hanging out.

We had decided to look for a rescue Lab, rather than raise a puppy again. We visited a local SPCA, had some 'get-to-know' time with a couple of rescues, to no avail. Then the Lake Erie Labrador Retriever Rescue caught our attention. We first saw Autumn on their website.

Autumn was housed at the Lawrence County Humane Society in New Castle, PA. One of their requirements was current household dogs needed to meet adoptees to determine their compatibility. Our visit went very well, so I brought Maggie near. Autumn laid down and showed her belly in submission—all was well in the world, and Autumn excitedly found herself traveling to her new home in Medina, Ohio, with a new name—Sophie.

On my return trip, Teresa called. "Did you see Autumn?" Teresa questioned. "Yes," I responded. "Well?" she asked.

Once home, the dogs immediately began playing, chasing, and running. Maggie taught Sophie how to frustrate me as I chipped golf balls for them to retrieve.

Sophie learned about walks, toys, that Maggie was top-dog, love for food, and two grandkids. Most importantly... that her new home was safe, and that she was loved.

When young kids are involved, there is a special concern about how they will get along, especially with a rescue.

Our grandkids loved Sophie. We began taking her on our annual family camping trips, and the grandchildren loved taking Sophie for walks.

Sophie's favorite activity was 1-3 hour walks at the local parks. Mostly everyone she met along the way was a friend. A few times, I heard a low rumble escape her throat as someone passed, and she wouldn't greet them. It made me wonder what she had experienced before she became part of our family. What was her life like? How was she treated? We found certain gestures caused her to flinch, so we avoided those. We also found scars on one side of her body; evidence she may have experienced some trauma.

The most remarkable thing was how loveable Sophie was. Our first Labrador, Sampson, was such a gentle, kind and loving soul that Teresa had put him on a pedestal—she loved him, and loved how he loved us back.

Sophie was rivaling this. For several years, Teresa repeatedly said, "She's such a good dog, but no one can take Sampson's crown." During the last few years of Sophie's time with us, Teresa finally declared..."It's hard for me to say, Sophie, but you have even passed Sampson up. You get the crown!"

Sophie lived with us for 8 ½ years. At the end, I took her to the vet due to a problem with her breathing. I asked them to contact me about her condition before they started any procedure. A little later, the vet's office called to inform me that they had to delay the procedure due to her breathing difficulty. I said, "I'm on my way."

Teresa met me there, and we realized it was time to say goodbye to Sophie—she was in serious trouble and declining quickly. It was a very difficult and emotional decision to make. She was so special and meant a great deal to our family.

Neither of us knew what to expect when we decided to get a rescue dog, but many of our friends and acquaintances told us the best dogs they knew were rescues. "They're so loving and grateful."

We found this to be true.

We're so glad for the day we saw Sophie's (Autumn's) picture on the LELRR website, and when Teresa asked, "Well?" I responded back with, "She's the one!" "I agree! She is the one!" she commented.

That's all I needed to hear. Sophie became an important and loved member of the family and changed our lives, as only a rescue can!

About Bob Arnold

Bob Arnold is an author, networker and architect. Bob simply believes in and has seen networking, whether in-person or a building facility and make phenomenal changes in people's lives and businesses. He specializes in "Anxiety Removal" and developing "Results-Oriented" directions in his networking partners and for his architectural clients. Bob's book, **The Uncanny Power of the Networking Pencil** is an international bestseller and has unlocked the secret power available as we network with purpose. He runs workshops, events and conferences centered on how networking is a necessary companion of effective leadership in today's workforce.

Bob and his wife Teresa loved having a rescue dog and their experience with Sophie affected their already deep love for dogs. Bob enjoys the outdoors immensely and takes their dogs on his walks in the woods.

You can reach out to Bob at TheNetworkingBob@gmail.com or go to his website www.OnwardNetworking.com and signup for his blog.

Dixie

True Blue Animal Rescue, located in Brenham, Texas, is a 501(c)(3) non-profit organization that takes in abused, neglected or abandoned animals, rehabilitates them, and finds them great new homes. Founded in January 2004, they are a no-kill shelter run by dedicated volunteers out of foster homes. They also provide support by spaying/neutering animals for people who could not otherwise afford to do so.

www.T-BAR.org

22

Our Sweet Dixie Girl

Sometimes we think Dixie Do-little rescued us. Do-little is the 15 year old Jack Russell Terrier who stole our hearts. By the way, we sometimes call Dixie "Do-little" because she doesn't do a lot!—though when she smiles, no one can command a room like she can.

Dixie came into our lives when she was about nine, not long after the 4th of July. The best we can surmise is that maybe fireworks scared her, and she got lost. It was evident that someone must have loved her, because she has a beautiful temperament, and responds well to requests. Unfortunately, when she was found she was malnourished, covered in fleas, had heart worms, and an enlarged heart.

When attempts to find her previous home failed, an email arrived from a friend, the cry of a person desperately looking to find Dixie a home. She had found Dixie outside a restaurant and had tried to have a shelter place her, but was turned down, classified as not adoptable because of the heart worms. Should my friend not have found a forever home for her by that weekend, Dixie would have been put down.

We were still grieving the loss of our dog which we had for ten years, so we really weren't planning on taking on an older, very sick dog this quickly, but one look at Dixie's picture changed our minds. They say "the eyes are the window to the soul." We knew the minute we saw Dixie's picture, we would be rescuing each other.

It is now six years to the day since Dixie Do-little came into our lives. Though she now also suffers from "Cushing's Disease," and we believe another potential tumor, she keeps on fighting, loving and stealing hearts, one by one. Did we mention that she has a part-time job?—yup, she is the Director of Guest Relations for our rental house, Bird Song Cottage, in Burton, Texas. She is such a good greeter, we practically have to pry our guests away from her. If we thought our guests were sweet on her, nothing compares with her special attachment to her Aunt Rozi, who looks in on her when we are out and about.

The days of Dixie climbing up on tables, only to jump down when she hears the key in the door, are gone. These days, she patiently awaits our arrival, curled up at the front door, with that welcoming smile and her loving eyes. Dixie is always happy to muster up the energy to stroll ever so slowly with us to the vegetable garden, still eager to snatch low-hanging tomatoes.

All is right with the world with Dixie by our side. Now, more than ever, we want her to savor every bit of joy she can find. Whether it's snuggling up with us in bed, having extra treats, or just basking in the sun on a beautiful day, we will never be able to thank her for all she has given us.

Forget the designer dogs, there is absolutely nothing better than a rescue dog; they don't ask for pedigree, why should we? We love you so much our sweet Dixie girl. Thank you for the joy you continue to bring us.

About Leslie Elhai

Leslie Elhai and her wife, Cathy Clark, are the owners of the Bird Song Cottage in Burton, Texas, just over the Round Top Texas line. Bird Song Cottage is a Texas Monthly Magazine-recommended cottage available for short-term rentals. Located equal distance between Houston and Austin, Texas, Round Top is home to the world-famous semi-annual antique shows, which have been known to draw over 150,000 people to this charming little town of 90 full-time residents.

The area is known for its galleries, restaurants, shops and performing arts venues. Home to the world-renowned Festival Hill Institute as well as the Junk Gypsy headquarters, Bird Song Cottage provides high-end accommodations for guests with discerning taste. Visit www.TheBirdSongCottage.com.

Dixie

"Love is a four-legged word."

Jager

Jager was adopted through Useless Bay Sanctuary, a non-profit 501(c)(3) registered charitable organization located in Seahurst, Washington. All Useless Bay Sanctuary volunteers are trained with a variety of techniques to capture stray dogs. They specialize in helping dogs that other people have struggled to catch. After a dog is rescued, Useless Bay Sanctuary actively searches for the dog owner for one month. At the end of one month, dogs that are not reunited are put up for adoption. Useless Bay Sanctuary screens each adoptive family through paperwork and a phone interview before introductions are made. Making a great match for each dog is important as they hope the dog finds their forever home.

www.UselessBaySanctuary.org

Fast Love

We had been looking to adopt another dog for several months when Jager's picture appeared on my computer screen. We already had a Golden Retriever, and were looking for a smaller companion dog; one that was big enough to play with her, but didn't take up as much space around the house. We had already been to a few adoption agencies, but just did not seem to be connecting with any dogs.

A woman at a local shelter was really upset when we did not adopt a dog on one of our visits. But if you have ever been somewhere to look at a dog, you know that they, in many ways, choose you. We had not met a dog that had done that yet.

Every morning, for the next few weeks, I would look to see what new dogs were posted for adoption. I kept clicking on this black male dog, labeled "Shepherd Mix." His ears were so big in the picture that I just assumed that he would be too big for our family.

One morning, I decided to take a chance and email the rescue group. As it turns out, he only weighed around 40 pounds, and was full grown. I requested a phone interview immediately. I was contacted by his foster dog mom just a few short days later. We had a great discussion about dogs and my family, and then she started to explain this particular dog. Several families had been out to see him and had already passed. He was just too fast.

I went out to visit with Jager where he was being fostered, and brought my daughter and Golden Retriever, Kona, with me. Right away, I knew this was going to work. He came out of the house and we took a walk with both dogs.

We returned to the fenced yard, and it was there that both dogs were let off leash. Kona is an aging dog, and is perfectly content sniffing and staying close to her humans. "Eleven," as he was named by his rescuer, was the fastest dog I have ever seen. He zoomed all over the yard at top speed, but would then return briefly to his foster mom's side, and occasionally mine. He repeated the "run and then hang out with humans" routine for several minutes while we talked. This was the dog we had hoped for the entire time. These minutes reminded me so much of when we picked out Kona in her litter as a puppy. They were both playful dogs who loved their people.

I called later that night, and told UBS we were interested in moving forward with the adoption process. A home visit was set up shortly after our conversation. While his foster dog mom was visiting and checking our home, I asked her why he was named "Eleven" in foster care. It was because the man who rescued him fell in love in eleven seconds. That is fast.

It probably took me about eleven seconds as well to fall in love with Jager. He is a young pup who has boundless energy and so much love to give. It pains me to think that no one was looking for him or didn't want to find him. My eyes well up with tears thinking about someone who didn't see what our family sees in him.

He wakes up every morning full of life and ready to tackle the day. He can chase tennis balls for hours, catch Frisbees out of the air (which my kids think is cool), swim at stealth speed, and then cuddle up right next to you.

I rarely enter a room by myself as he is constantly at my heels. When I fold laundry, he sits on the pile and licks my face. When I take my truck keys off the hook, he runs to the garage. When someone isn't feeling well, he is sitting right next to them. He was quick to pick up on life in our home, and made his way quickly into our hearts. Jager is the ultimate second chance dog, and we are so thankful he chose us.

About Jennifer Lee

Jennifer Lee is a teacher in the White River School District. She has a Bachelor's Degree in Elementary Education from Washington State University (Go Cougs!), a Master's Degree in Creative Arts Education from Lesley University, and achieved National Board Certification in Reading-Language Arts. Jennifer has taught a variety of grade levels. She is restarting her career in education after spending several years at home raising her children. Jennifer lives in Washington State and is married to her high school sweetheart, Travis. They have two children, Carson and Whitney, along with their two dogs, Kona and Jager. She enjoys reading, being outdoors in the Pacific Northwest, camping, Cougar football games, and traveling.

You can contact Jennifer by email at jened110@gmail.com.

Prince

When Texas-based Austin Pets Alive! started rescuing animals in 2008, Austin was somewhat rich in resources that prevented births. For almost ten years, more and more resources were put into spay and neuter programs, but the live outcome rate at our city shelter was stuck around 50%. Of course, the population of Austin was quickly growing, so it's likely that the spay and neuter resources were helping our live outcome rate from getting worse.

By developing comprehensive, innovative programs that targeted these key groups of animals and pulling directly from euthanasia lists, Austin Pets Alive! has saved more than 50,000 dogs and cats since 2008.

www.AustinPetsAlive.org

Bobby-Prince and the Morning Miracle

This story begins on a beautiful early November morning in 2015. I work from home and have a morning routine that includes walking two miles in my neighborhood. I almost always complete this walk before 8 am, but on this day I became consumed by a task, and it was already 10 am when I realized I hadn't gone walking. I put on my walking shoes and was heading to the front door when I sat down and told myself it was already too late. Then, within a minute, I just changed my mind and started walking.

When I was about a half mile away from arriving back home, I heard something behind me. I turned around and saw a little tan and furry dog following me. I sprinted for about 200 meters to lose him, but when I stopped to catch my breath, he was right by my feet and looking at me like he was saying, "is that all you have?" I didn't want him to run into the road and get hurt, so I picked him up and walked home.

Our house already had three cats that ruled the space, but this little dog wasn't intimidated, even though he was about the same size as our biggest cat. Our neighborhood doesn't allow fences, so we couldn't just leave him outside in our yard, and our city has a no-leash law for dogs.

We never saw any lost dog signs in the area, and the vet said he did not have a microchip. We are fortunate to live in Austin, Texas, which happens to be the largest no-kill city in the country. It's led by the efforts of many great people at Austin Pets Alive! It made us happy to know that if we had to take him there, he would have a chance to get adopted and live a great life. It was never an option for us to keep him, since one dog and three cats in a small house is not a good long-term situation. At this point, we named him Bobby, but we knew his forever family might rename him.

About this time, we remembered that my wife's cousin, Michelle, and her family had lost their long-time dog to old age a few years before. We sent her some photos and videos of Bobby, and she talked it over with her husband, Michael. They decided to adopt Bobby and give him a forever home.

We had him groomed, neutered, and vaccinated before we met Michelle to give him to her. It was a couple of weeks before Christmas, and Michelle surprised her two kids with this early Christmas gift. They renamed him Prince. It is a perfect name, because he lives like royalty with a great family that loves him dearly.

I often think finding Prince was a small miracle. Something made me go walking that morning, even though in my mind it was already too late in the day. Our only goal was to find him a forever home and give him every possibility to live a long and fun life surrounded by people that love him. He was even one of the reasons why I decided to become a volunteer at Austin Pets Alive!

Here is Michelle's retelling of the story:

After losing our dog, Princess, we decided that we would get another pet when the "right dog came along at the right time." We were not actively looking for this next pet, when Frank contacted us about the little dog he and his wife rescued... but guess what? This little dog was meant to be a member of our family from day one. My kids both cried tears of joy when I arrived home with him, and they gave him the name Prince, because he looked so much like our previous dog, Princess.

Life with Prince is great. He loves car rides, going on

walks, and chasing you around in the backyard. He's energetic yet doesn't hesitate to curl up next to you when it's time for bed. My husband runs his own business from our home, and he is the perfect greeter for our customers. We are so blessed that he came into our lives, and when people ask what kind of dog he is, my first response is always "the best kind -- a rescued one."

About Frank Zuniga

Frank Zuniga is a retired Army officer with more than 28 years of service. He is now an entrepreneur in both commercial and residential real estate and he is also a licensed realtor in Texas. He is passionate about showing people about other opportunities that exist for selling or buying a home besides traditional methods. When people have more than one way to reach their goals that means more freedom and leads to other benefits.

When not working on real estate, you'll find Frank working on self-improvement and social media marketing. He also an avid walker and nature lover. He volunteers at the Austin Pets Alive! animal shelter which has led the way in earning Austin, Texas, the title as the largest no-kill city in the country.

You can contact Frank by email at frank@frankzunigahq.com or visit his website at www.FrankZunigaHQ.com.

Pearl & Mattie

Pearl and Mattie were both adopted from the Animal Protection Society of Caswell County in Yanceyville, North Carolina (APS Caswell). It is a non-profit organization that operates the local animal shelter for the county. APS Caswell is fortunate to have two full-time and several part-time staff members, who are supported by a group of dedicated volunteers and supporters. APS Caswell provides a host of low cost or free services to the community, including rabies vaccinations, coordination with spay and neuter clinics, medical care for shelter animals, coordination with rescue groups and foster homes, adoption processing, etc. The group relies heavily on financial contributions and donations of food and supplies, and maintains a 'Dog and Cat Wish List' on their web site.

www.APSCaswell.org

25

It's All a Black & White Issue:
We All Need Rescuing

It was the first week of January, and we were in the grips of the coldest winter weather we had experienced in years. Late one frigid Sunday night, some heartless soul dropped a basket of puppies over the fence at our local animal shelter. When staff arrived for work, they found eight shivering little Labrador Retriever pups – four black, three chocolate, and one white.

Always at near capacity, the shelter's manager started working the phones, calling individuals they hoped would agree to foster one or more of the puppies for a few days. Finding a permanent home for them would not be a problem, but in the short term they simply needed reliable and safe places for them to stay. My wife Tracy received one of the calls, and immediately headed to the shelter to help.

The first I learned of this situation was when I arrived home from the office later that afternoon, only to find Tracy and our youngest daughter (home from college for a few days) huddled on the den floor with a white ball of fur – along with Millie, our full-grown Black Lab, watching over them like a proud aunt. Tracy's first words were, "It's only temporary, and for just a few days until the shelter can place the puppies in permanent homes." I thought one dog was enough for our busy home, but how could I protest too much under the circumstances?

Little did I know a conspiracy must have been in the works. As I sat in my study a little later, I felt a tug at one of my slippers...a gentle nudge that shortly became an all-out tug-of-war, moving from right foot to left. And the next night it was more of the same, and reports from the family indicated the little white blur was in constant motion about the house – except when napping in her 'new' quilt. I restated my opinion that one dog was enough, and my wife and daughter agreed (or so I thought).

By Wednesday night I had had enough. One slipper was completely destroyed, and the tugging at my feet had grown into a tugging at my heart. So, when I stomped through the den on my way to the kitchen, I stopped and proclaimed, "If the dog is going to stay with us, we cannot just call her 'Puppy.' She must have a name...which will be Pearl. Besides, Millie needs a playmate, and there will be no further discussion, so do not try to change my mind."

At this point I need to pause, take a slight story detour and confess that Pearl was not our first 'rescue' pet, nor was Millie. Our first rescue was more or less a simple case of accidental adoption. My wife was a walker/runner for years, and one day as she trotted along, a little black puppy appeared, and took up the run beside her. Keeping time step by step, the pup stayed with Tracy all the way home. After we exhausted efforts over the next few days to find any owner or home from which she was missing, 'Sassy' was officially welcomed into our family.

Sassy ran with Tracy each day, but I never took much interest in her as I was occupied with our girls, my business, helping dad on the farm, etc. Truth be told, I had never been much of a pet person. Growing up we had dogs on the farm, but not as pets such as Sassy was to Tracy...and wanted to be with me.

Sadly, Sassy was not with us for long. She became sickly one week, right before we left on a planned trip to the mountains, so we left Sassy in the care of a local vet. I use the term 'care' loosely, for when we returned we were informed that Sassy had passed away during our absence. I will not dwell on what happened, just use this as a word of caution to choose your vet carefully.

Our next rescue experience began on a much more adventurous note. I was looking at a rental house with our oldest daughter when we were surprised by her mother pulling into the driveway. Upon opening the car door, out jumped what seemed to be a Black Lab as big as a bear... who took off for parts unknown. Luckily, and I mean that literally, as we were in the middle of a congested neighborhood in town, Tracy caught up with 'the beast' four streets away after a chase over several blocks.

This was how Millie (short for Millicent) immersed herself into our lives. Tracy had rescued this two-year old Black Lab from a home where she was kept inside all the time, which was not what this creature full of energy needed.

Once we got Millie out on the farm, she quickly became 'our' dog. She would spend time playing in the yard and the daily walk/run with Tracy, but also became my constant companion as I tended the cows, walked fence lines, worked in the hay fields, or simply crossed the field to visit my mom and dad.

But as much as we grew to love Millie, it soon became obvious she needed a companion, a playmate, a friend. And although we had thought about this for a while, with Tracy visiting the shelter and scanning the paper hoping for a sign of the ideal brother or sister for Millie, no sign was received – until that Monday morning call that brought Pearl to us.

Picking back up where I left off, I returned down the hall to my study, knowing our days were going to be all the richer with Pearl in our family. And richer they were. Pearl and Millie became fast best friends, spending their days together outside, and making our home more peaceful and loving each evening (after we got Pearl through the puppy stage, which only took 2-3 years).

There is so much more that could be said, so many more memories that could be shared, but those will have to wait for another time. And time, ever fleeting in hindsight, is not infinite, as we were to find out much too soon. Pearl was diagnosed with mouth cancer in early 2015, and we made the heart-breaking decision to release her to cross over the Rainbow Bridge in July of that year. A few months later, I came home from work one afternoon, and wondered why Millie did not greet me at our back yard fence, as was her habit. I found her sleeping under her favorite shade tree outside our sunroom, still warm – but gone from us forever.

The emptiness in our home and hearts was huge, and we promised each other not to get another dog for a while, if ever. While the joy they bring is endless, the pain that lingers when they leave is deep and evident at every turn.

But life moves forward, and we adapt and change and rethink priorities. And before I knew it, Tracy began secretly going by the shelter every week or two, and suddenly there is another Black Lab lying at my feet each night. Mattie (short for Matilda) has her own personality and quirks, but when she places her head across my leg and stares longingly into my eyes, it is almost as if she knows that she has filled a void in our home...and our hearts.

And we have once again been rescued. What a great feeling.

About Dwight O. Chandler

Dwight O. Chandler is President/Owner of The Chandler Marketing Group, a marketing, advertising, communications and publishing firm. With over 38 years of experience, Mr. Chandler has comprehensive knowledge in all aspects of the industry, specializing in marketing and advertising consulting, conceptual thinking, copywriting, and corporate communications. He is currently serving as Chief Operations Officer for The TES Group, a leading special events services company serving the eastern United States.

Dwight is also a published author and illustrator and is currently working on a series of books to be published beginning in late 2018 or early 2019. Aside from his regular work, he spends what little 'free' time he has with his wife of 37 years (the true dog-lover and rescuer in the family), working on his family's farm, writing and drawing, and enjoying his three grandchildren.

Contact Dwight at: dchandler@chandlermarketinggroup.com or dchandler214@yahoo.com.

Milly & Rufus

Milly and Rufus were adopted from two different non-profit 501(c)(3) animal shelters. Milly was adopted from the Livingston County Humane Society in Howell, Michigan. Before her adoption, Milly was fortunate enough to have been placed in their foster program for five months and was adopted directly out of it. Rufus was adopted from the Huron Valley Humane Society located in Ann Arbor, Michigan. He was transferred to Huron Valley from a shelter in North Carolina where he was originally taken in, but after no luck of being adopted, they decided it was time for him to find a fresh start and transferred him to Huron Valley.

www.Humane-Livingston.org

www.HSHV.org

26

The Most Unexpected Best Friends

My boyfriend, Aaron, and I took a leap of faith with each other two and a half years ago and adopted Milly and Rufus. I had never been around dogs and didn't know if I was a "dog person," but I knew how much he had wanted one after being separated from his childhood dog when his parents divorced. When he told me about Milly and her heartbreaking story, I knew we had to adopt her, but what I didn't know is that we were going to adopt Rufus the same day!

Milly is the sweetest little 12-year-old beagle anyone could ever meet. Her hobbies include cuddling, sunbathing, and snacking. Before being brought into rescue, Milly had spent most of her time tied to a tree outside and was abandoned by her previous owner with no food or water in a house with four other dogs for over two weeks. She chewed through drywall and damaged most of her teeth during that time. When we adopted her, she was 15 pounds underweight, and was heartworm positive. Because Milly was an older dog and severely underweight, multiple vets discouraged performing any heartworm treatment. However, after us giving Milly her monthly heartworm preventative for eight months, she was tested heartworm negative! We continue to give Milly her monthly preventative, and she is now a healthy 10 pounds overweight.

We were shocked that we were able to take Milly home the same day we went to visit her and fill out the paperwork! However, because we were unsure if we would be the family selected to adopt Milly, we had already decided to go meet another dog at Huron Valley Humane Society that day, and we decided to keep the appointment. We wanted to at least give the dog some love and attention for a bit.

When we got there, the dog we had arranged to meet ended up not being ready for adoption just yet. Of course, that didn't stop us from saying hi to every other dog that was in there. We had said hi to almost all the dogs, and there was one that Aaron insisted they take out of his kennel to say hello to. I'm not sure how Aaron knew this was the dog he had to meet; it must have been intuition mixed with fate.

This dog was well overdue for a bath, shaking with fear, and looked like he hadn't slept in days. I'll be honest, he looked like a dog most people would pass over and be disgusted by. We learned that this was the second shelter this dog had been at trying to find his forever home. He had already been adopted and brought back twice because they said he was aggressive. Aaron and I couldn't help but laugh when they said that, because this dog only had seven teeth total in his mouth! Due to his lack of teeth, his tongue hangs out the right side of his mouth constantly, but it's the cutest, and he gets plenty of attention because of it when we go to the park! Besides hanging his tongue out, Rufus' only other hobby is getting into as much mischief as possible.

We decided that there was no way we could leave him behind. We ended up naming the dog Rufus that night. It took three months of Aaron sleeping on the floor next to his crate to calm him down at night, a year of all hands-on-deck potty training, and continuous training to this day to get Rufus adjusted to living with us. Milly supported him during the process, and still does. She mothers Rufus when he gets out of line or becomes aggressive, checks on him when he's in time out, and cuddles him when he is scared.

We are amazed at how instantly bonded Milly and Rufus became. They are the best of friends. They are constantly looking for each other, engaging in mini Wrestle-Mania sessions, going for walks and barking at our neighbors together, sharing an ice-cream cone, and cuddling up next to each other for nap time.

Every day Aaron and I reflect on how blessed we are that the four of us were brought together as family. They are the best part of our day and made us realize how precious every second of the day is. We are grateful that we were provided with the resources to give them a fun and loving home.

About Nina Drumsta

Nina Drumsta is the Content Marketing Manager at Child Care Marketing Solutions. Nina and her team have a mission to provide industry-leading early childhood business coaching and training. Through this they hope to positively impact the lives of one million children through transforming 5,000 early learning businesses. Nina is happy to contribute her skill set for a team that comes to work every day ready to make a positive impact in the lives of their clients and demonstrates passion daily. Please visit childcare-marketing.com for more information or if you are interested in their products and coaching services.

When Nina isn't working, her favorite activity is spending all the time she can with her fur babies and their dad. She also enjoys a good cup of coffee and feeding her Pinterest addiction by being an avid crafter of many crafts.

Nina can be contacted directly at ninadrumsta@gmail.com.

About Dog Joy Books

Dog Joy Books is a book publisher dedicated to helping dog rescue organizations raise awareness and funds through the publishing of unique storytelling books like the one you are holding right now. These effective fund-raising books provide rescue organizations and shelters a powerful and unique way to raise money and awareness with **no upfront costs** to your organization. Dog Joy Books removes the tedious and difficult work of publishing a book and gives rescue organizations an easy and simple way to create an effective marketing and publicity tool to share within their community.

Sharing dog rescue success stories from your own organization is a compelling and dynamic way to let others know about the important service you provide within your community so that you can save more dogs. It also gives your clients' a fun way to share their own dog's story with the world.

For more details about how you can publish your own Dog Joy edition(s), visit www.DogJoyBooks.com.